Hereditary Traits

Breaking the Destructive Cycle of Hereditary Influence

Bill Basansky, Ph.D.

LONGWOOD
COMMUNICATIONS

Published by:
Longwood Communications
1310 Alberta Street
Longwood, FL 32750
407-260-0016

All Scripture quotations are from the King James Version of
the Holy Bible.

To order additional copies or to have Dr. Basansky speak to
your group, write to:

Love and Grace Fellowship, Inc.
P.O. Box 7126
Fort Myers, FL 33911-7126
Phone: 813-768-1300

DEDICATION

This book is lovingly dedicated to my darling wife, Bea, my partner and best friend, for her encouragement and support of my ministry.

I also dedicate this work to my wonderful sons Eric and Jerry and their families, and to my mother, who prayed for and believed in me.

Special thanks go to my Associate Pastor, Ramon Duvall, and my Administrator, Carmen Shafer, who are my true friends; they have exemplified loyalty and faithfulness like no others I know.

CONTENTS

FOREWORD

Since birth, you have been learning to be you; behavior is learned in the first social setting of home, among family and playmates. You have grown into the complex symphony of behaviors that you are today.

Have you tried to change your life for the better and stand up for your rights only to find that you have driven away your friends, antagonized people you work with and alienated your mate and children? You are not alone. This book offers an effective way to turn things around and unlearn poor habits, breaking the patterns of destructive hereditary traits and replacing them with positive action. You'll find practical exercises for making beneficial and lasting changes in your life.

Social behaviors, language behaviors, communication behaviors, conflict behaviors, affection behaviors—all are learned from models we have observed and interaction we have witnessed among parents, siblings and family—like parent, like child.

It takes two to continue destructive inherited behavior in a relationship, but it takes only one to end it. First, this book will help you discern where you are spiritually. Then, after you have "located" yourself, it will help you to grow and mature into a deeper and better stage of spiritual development. In the process, you'll shed old behaviors and learn to encourage Christ-centered relationships.

INTRODUCTION

Many of the diseases, behaviors, characteristics and habits that are commonly called hereditary are caused by spirits that have attached themselves to a particular family or group.

Spirits do not die. People die, but the spirits live on and on, perpetuating the same problems, habits and attitudes in members of a family.

Demons are disembodied beings. They are looking for bodies in which to do their father's will. Their father is the devil, whose job is to steal, kill and destroy.

Spirits will continue to create problems in a person's life or in the lives of loved ones until they are recognized for what they are and defeated with the Word of God. Why do you think the Bible instructs us in James 4:7 to "submit [ourselves] therefore to God.

Resist the devil, and he will flee from [us]"?

Hereditary condition is often used to explain a particular behavior in a person's life when in fact it is a familiar spirit that has been passed on in the family from generation to generation. As a matter of fact, the Bible says in Exodus 34:7 that the sins of the fathers are passed on to their children and their children's children up to the fourth generation.

Familiar spirits are mentioned in the Old Testament as evil spirits. The Israelites were forbidden by God to have any association with them. Anyone who operated in a familiar spirit was to be stoned to death. In the New Testament Jesus teaches us to cast them out of people.

So let's ask ourselves these questions: What are familiar spirits? What do they do? How do they act? What does the Bible say about them? And when they do get in, how can you cast them out?

Familiar spirits are "familiar" with a person, place or thing. They are the spirits who are familiar with you. They know about you because they have lived with you and around you long enough to become familiar with you. Since they know all about you, they know exactly what it takes to make you feel inadequate. They know how to make you feel rejected. They know what will make you withdraw. They know what will make you want to give up and quit. They will use this knowledge to try to defeat you in life.

Even as a Christian, once you've been set free, the Bible says in Genesis 4:6-7 that sin lies at the door, meaning that the devil has assigned demons to follow you and become familiar with everything that disturbs you. When the time is right, they manifest themselves or set up a situation to which they know you will react in a certain way (see 2 Timothy 2:24-26).

Spirits are passed down from one member of the family or from a member of a closely related group to another. Babies or children (biological children as well as spiritual children) have very little resistance, and it is relatively easy for a spirit to attach itself to a child unless someone is covering that child with prayer.

When you begin to examine behavior or characteristics in family groups who are associated closely, you will be amazed to see the same general group of spirits operating in their lives through rebellion, strife, jealousy, fear of darkness, habits of alcoholism, drug addiction, migraine headaches, epilepsy and self-pity. Learn how to deal with these specific spirits through the Word of God rather than merely battle the symptoms.

To remove the spirit you first have to identify the spirit, locate and eradicate it, or, as the Bible says, cast it out of the person.

When these familiar behaviors or characteristics manifest themselves in your children's lives, remember it is a spirit in operation. You must take control of them or your loved ones will end up with the same set of problems you have. Many times these problems will be even more severe, as they multiply in greater numbers.

Spirits are always the same; they do not change from one generation to another. Some of the spirits are manifested more frequently than others through rebellion and insecurity. In fact, these spirits are so prevalent that I have added a section in this book to help you identify them and cast them out.

The Bible forbids Christians to have anything to do with familiar spirits. The King James Version of the Bible mentions familiar spirits in the Old Testament more than fifteen times. Since they are mentioned only in the Old Testament, does this mean they have been done away with? Have they ceased to exist? Have they become extinct? Are they no longer operating today? How do they get into your life? When do they get in? These are some of the questions we will look at as we search God's Word together for the answers on how to defeat the spirits that have become familiar with you and how you can be free from them.

All evil spirits have a purpose and a goal in mind. Their ultimate goal is to defeat you and destroy you. They are determined to keep you down, to make you feel inadequate, helpless, unworthy and inferior. They bring sickness, poverty, grief and every other evil thing to you. Many times they will operate in arrogance through haughty know-it-all spirits. They will try to wreck your life. They will try to bring grief and destruction into your life.

The term *familiar spirit* refers to a spirit of divination or its medium or conjurer. Originally it meant the ritual hole or pit dug in the ground to give underworld spirits access to the practitioner for short periods of time. Later the term was applied to the spirits which issued from the hole as well as to the necromancer.

A necromancer is one who calls up ghosts or spirits to reveal the future, or one who speaks to the dead. The term *familiar* is used to describe the alleged spirit of a deceased person or a spirit belonging to the family. Thus, it was on intimate terms with the deceased person and was familiar with that person's habits.

A parallel term in Hebrew means "to know." A knowing spirit, one with occult power, acknowledges a wizard, who is made wise by contacting the nether world by such a demon. Deuteronomy 18:11 indicates that the same medium might consult a familiar spirit as well as a knowing spirit.

One of the most descriptive accounts in the Old Testament is in 1 Samuel 28 where Saul sought the counsel of a witch to try to contact Samuel, who was dead. The witch of Endor was the mistress of a familiar spirit. She was expected to call up that spirit—a controlled spirit. When Samuel appeared instead of her familiar controlled spirit, the witch was astonished and frightened. It was only then that she recognized Saul as the king.

Contacting a familiar spirit was one of the reasons why Saul was destroyed. The punishment for breaking or ignoring God's law is great. Sometimes mediums, witches, conjurers, wizards and fortunetellers really do work with familiar, or controlled spirits. Since the spirits are familiar with a person, place or thing, sometimes they do have knowledge of a particular person, place or thing. Not everyone who has supernatural knowledge about you is necessarily of God. Familiar spirits have knowledge about you, and they communicate this knowledge to those whom they serve. Don't let this upset you. God gives us standards by which to judge prophecy. Surely you would not go to a fortuneteller, wizard, palmist, magician or hypnotist, would you? You have the Word of God. When you apply God's standard to situations or people in your life, you will not be fooled.

In the spirit world your life is like an open book. So don't be surprised if someone reads a chapter or two in your book and tells you things he has no natural way of knowing. The Bible instructs us in Matthew 7:15-20 to be fruit inspectors, to examine the fruit in the lives of those people who are predicting or prophesying to you. If their fruit is rotten, you will have no problem determining their source of information.

It is impossible for a spiritualist, medium, necromancer or even a prophet of the Lord to speak to the dead, but you can speak to a spirit. God is a spirit. (See John 4:24.) So is the devil. Therefore, the deceiver speaks to, and gets his information from, spirits who are familiar with a particular person or situation. When you examine Scripture you will understand that people cannot call up or speak to a deceased person's spirit. Paul, by the inspiration of the Holy Spirit, wrote in 2 Corinthians 5:8, "To be absent from the body [is] to be present with the Lord."

In Ecclesiastes 12:7 the Holy Spirit recorded, "Then shall the dust return to the earth as it was: and the spirit shall return unto God who gave it."

It is clear from Luke 16:19-31 that no person or thing has the right or power to do anything with your spirit except God. When your body goes to the grave, your spirit (the real you) goes to be with the Lord or with the devil.

Many times Christians have asked: Does the devil know what you are thinking? Can he read your mind? The only time the devil can read your mind is when he plants something in your mind. Does he know what you think? He only knows how you react to the things he puts in your mind. He knows that with certain stimuli you will react in certain ways. Let's explore this question by looking at familiar spirits and how they work.

Familiar spirits know how you act, and they know how you react to almost every situation. They know about you because they have lived with you or around you for years. They have lived in your family, they have lived with your ancestors. They know how the family conducts itself. They know exactly which buttons to push to get you to act or react in a certain way.

Philippians 2:5 says, "Let this mind be in you, which was also in Christ Jesus." The devil could not read Jesus' mind. Neither will he be able to read your mind when it is renewed and stayed in the Word of God. First Corinthians 2:11 says, "For what man knoweth the things of a man, save the spirit of man which is in him?" If the Spirit of God controls and guides your life, and your mind is stayed on the things of God, then the devil cannot control your mind.

In Philippians 4:8 the Bible says, "Finally, brethren, whatsoever things are true,...honest,... just,... pure,... lovely,... [and] of good report; if there be any virtue, and if there be any praise, think on these things." You cannot think correctly and act wrongly, nor can you think wrongly and act correctly, for every tree brings forth its own fruit. Therefore, whatever you think on, that's what you're going to be, and you will yield yourself to that spirit (Romans 7:15-25).

The only information the devil has about you is what your lifestyle has been in the past, the way you are living now and what you tell him with your mouth. Your actions and your tongue give you away every time. Reporting to the devil is a spirit who is familiar with you, and when this spirit sees you react to certain situations the same way time and time again, he is fairly certain you will react the same way the next time. So he lays the trap.

14

Some of you try to fool him the same way you try to fool your spouse or perhaps even your church. For example, suppose you hear a message on confession and you are sick and want to be healed. Remembering Isaiah 53, you confess that you are healed. Thank God confession does bring possession when you believe in your heart. Maybe you stand up to give a testimony and say, "I believe every word in the Bible. I believe the Bible from cover to cover, from Genesis to Revelation. I believe that by Jesus' stripes I am healed." But at the first pain you run home, fall on your bed, pull the covers over your head and sob. Why? You have not fooled the devil. He has you figured out, and you can be certain he will continue to use you for target practice because he still has the same old familiar spirit reporting the damaging effects his fiery darts are having on your life.

Familiar spirits oftentimes camouflage themselves with words such as *hereditary* and *genetic*. A synonym for hereditary is *innate*, and the word hereditary comes from the Latin word *hareditarius*. It has several meanings:
1. Passed down by inheritance from an ancestor to a legal heir.
2. Passed down by heredity; designating, or of a characteristic transmitted from generation to generation.
3. Being such because of attitudes, beliefs, etc., passed down through generations.

Heredity means the transmission of characteristics from parents to offspring. Characteristics, behavior and attitudes are learned; therefore, they are not part of you at birth, whereas genes are. Even the dictionaries do not list *heredity* and *genetics* as synonyms, therefore it is clear that they are two different entities and have two different functions.

Genes are transmitted from parent to offspring by means of chromosomes. They belong to you at birth. The tendency of offspring is to resemble parents or ancestors through such transmission. For example, if parents have blue eyes, the chance is good the child will also have blue eyes. If a parent or parents have blond or dark hair, it is probable that the child receiving those genes will also have blond or dark hair, whichever the case may be. Anything that you can inherit from another, you can also refuse. Genes cannot be refused. They are part of you. But whatever traits or characteristics your ancestors possessed that you do not want, you do not have to accept. You can free yourself from any of those attachments which are caused by familiar spirits or any other evil spirit. You can take authority over that condition or that demon, break its power or the curse that's upon your life and drive it out of your life or your loved one's life with the authority of the Word of God and in the name of Jesus.

James 4:7-8 says, "Submit yourselves therefore to God. Resist the devil, and he will flee from you. Draw nigh to God, and he will draw nigh to you." Mark 16:17-18 says, "And these signs shall follow them that believe; In my name shall they cast out devils;...they shall lay hands on the sick, and they shall recover."

CHAPTER ONE

Transference and Counter-Transference of Spirits

To fully understand transference and counter-transference of spirits, we must go to the Word of God as our source. We will also examine teaching from well-known authors and professionals, but we will go to the ultimate expert, Jesus, to find out what He has to say. Humanists do not consider human beings to be trichotomous, or comprised of three parts. They consider humans to be dichotomous—two-part beings. The Bible teaches that we have a spirit, a soul and a body. We are triune beings formed in the image and likeness of God.

To understand this fully, look at 1 Corinthians 2:11-14, which deals with areas that will be very informative, namely transference and counter-transference of spirits.

A therapist or counselor who does not understand spiritual things will listen to what a patient wants to communicate. He can identify with that particular patient's thoughts, desires, moods and feelings, surrendering in a free association with the person. In other words, he has compassion for the patient and relates to what the patient is saying. In so doing, he opens himself up to receive what the patient has to say, good or bad. He is then open to receive the person's spirit. A transference and counter-transference takes place.

The counselor has to open himself up freely. He has to have feeling and compassion for the patient. This is why Jesus said, "Come unto me, all ye that labour and are heavy laden, and I will give you rest" (Matt. 11:28). You may not realize what is happening, but there are transferences and counter-transferences taking place. Jesus takes your burden and He sets you free. He says, "Put all your burdens on me, because I care for you."

The only One who can carry your burden is Jesus Christ. If you do not understand this concept, you will never have a true answer. If a counselor is not equipped with this knowledge, he faces a great danger in transference. A counselor is not to receive the patient's problems or burdens or receive any of what the patient has. The counselor is there merely as a conduit that all of the problems will go through to Jesus. If it does not go that way, the counselor is in trouble.

There is tremendous danger involved. All the counselors who are not equipped with spiritual knowledge become a dam. When a river is dammed up, the pressure builds against the dam. If there is too much pressure the dam will break. If you are a counselor and there is too much pressure against you, and you become the spiritual dam (whereby you block off or receive another person's problems), before long those pressures will cause you (the dam) to break. That is why oftentimes people break. Their will and their power are not strong enough to withstand the supernatural powers.

Sooner or later the therapist will respond in counter-transference. He will become anxious, discouraged, annoyed, disappointed and despairing of life. He will arrive at the point where he will say, "What's the use? It's not worth it. I can't take it anymore."

Do you know people like that? Do you know what is happening? They absorb all the problems into themselves. They are saturated and find no way for themselves. If they do not have the answer, they will break under the pressure. It will make them do things they would never do under normal circumstances. But under pressure they will do anything to get out of it. They may regret their actions later, but they cannot turn back.

Transference and counter-transference then become detrimental to the counselor or therapist. Even though counseling and therapy are good, if you do not know how to relieve yourself of the problems, it will harm you. Food is good, but too much of it can be harmful to you. Water is good, but you can drown in it if you do not know how to swim or if you do not use wisdom.

Qualities of Effective Counselors

It is important for you as a counselor, before doing anything, to ask the Holy Spirit to give you direction that you will have the compassion and wisdom of Christ and not be trapped by pity parties the devil is going to bring through other people because he is after you. He is not so much after the counselee; he is after the counselor. He is not so much after the people in the church; he is after the pastor. He is not after the people in the nation; he is after the president of the nation. If the leader is thrown out of the way, the sheep will scatter.

This must be applied not only in counseling situations but also in everyday living. It must be applied in your family relationships, your business, your marriage and your relationships with other people. You are God's ambassador; however, you are not to become a problem-carrier.

Heinrich Rackur of Germany is an expert on this subject. He speaks of the reality of transference and counter-transference that takes place between a patient and a counselor. This, he says, is the way it is supposed to be done. In order for the counselee to open up to you as a counselor, he has to feel you are sympathetic to his cause and are on his side. The danger, as I have already explained, is when you take the position of being God, as having all the answers when you do not have them. We do not have solutions unless we have the solution-solver, Jesus. One human being really cannot help another human being. It is like the blind leading the blind. You both end up in a ditch! Some people are intellectually wiser than others and through experience have learned certain ways that have worked temporarily, but only temporarily. What is needed is a permanent solution. The permanent solution can be found only in Jesus Christ.

Freudian disciples do not believe in spiritual things, and that is why they are not successful in their approach. They have been in practice for quite some time, and we still have thousands of people in mental institutions who have not been helped. As a matter of fact, those people are sent to mental institutions by the Freudian disciples.

Counter-transference and transference do occur but should happen in the right fashion, and the only right way is God's way. Any other way is contrary to the Word.

Matthew 11:28 says, "Come unto me, all ye that labour and are heavy laden, and I will give you rest." Jesus is the only One who can give you rest. In other words, those who are heavy laden, oppressed, weighted with problems, come unto Jesus. Verse 29 says, "Take my yoke upon you, and learn of me; for I am meek and lowly in heart: and ye shall find rest unto your souls." Now watch! He said you will find rest unto your souls—your mind, your will, your emotions, your feelings. He says you will find, for your soul, that peace of mind in Him: not in a psychiatrist, not in medicine, not in psychologists, but in Him. God can use psychologists and psychiatrists, and He uses medicine. That's great! However, He said the ultimate answer is in Him.

It is suggested that the counselor's total response is decisive for the understanding and interpretation of the patient's psychological process. It is important for a counselor to understand the psychological process. How can you understand a psychological process when you do not understand the spiritual process? You will never understand a psychological process or what causes a person to think good or bad if you do not understand that there is a spirit motivating these people.

Matthew 11:30 says, "For my yoke is easy, and my burden is light." In order for us to understand, Jesus is speaking in parables. If you were living in those days, you would understand perfectly what He is saying. When you yoke someone to you, you become the lead. For example, with a team of oxen, the leading ox will have the yoke. That ox takes the burden and pulls the plow. The ox that is yoked to him stays a little behind, and all of the weight is upon the leading ox, not the ox who follows. When you are yoked to Jesus and He leads you, all of the burden is upon Him. The only thing you do is attach yourself to Him. He does all the work. You just go along beside Him. You do not get tired because He leads you and takes care of all the responsibilities of work. Jesus says, "My yoke is easy, and My burden is light. I'm not going to make you do all the pulling. I'll take care of you." If I say I am going to take your problems—I am going to help you—then we become yoke-bearers. We become the ones who will carry the burden, and Jesus says that is not the way.

One more passage I would like you to read is John 7:37-39, where it says, "In the last day, that great day of the feast, Jesus stood and cried, saying, If any man thirst, let him come unto me, and drink" (v. 37). He could have said, "If any man is hungry, let him come unto Me and eat. If any man is burdened, let him come unto Me and receive help. If any man is sick, let him come unto Me and receive healing. If any man is oppressed, let him come unto Me and receive deliverance. If any man, any human being, has any need, let him come to Me. I am the answer." Jesus is saying to us, "Come to Me, and I will give you rest."

Now He goes on to say in verses 38-39, "He that believeth on me, as the Scripture hath said, out of his belly shall flow rivers of living water. (But this spake he of the Spirit, which they that believe on him should receive: for the Holy Ghost was not yet given; because that Jesus was not yet glorified.)"

"...Out of [your] belly shall flow rivers of living water. (But this spake he of the Spirit...)." Now we are coming to something very important, because before that time the Holy Spirit was not yet given. The people did not know anything about the Holy Spirit. Suddenly He introduces a Spirit, the Holy Spirit of God. He says that when you have the Holy Spirit inside of you, He will guide you into all truth and set you free.

Let's ask ourselves this question: If any counselor is dealing with a demon-possessed person and transference takes place, how does he repress such a transference if he does not believe that demons exist or that their spirits exist? How can you or anyone else who does not believe in spiritual beings help that person?

For example, if the patient is hostile and the counselor opens himself up in an attempt to reach the patient, that counselor also opens himself to counter-transference of the spirit that caused the patient's hostile behavior. If he does not understand there is a spirit at work, he may start acting just like the patient.

Demonic control or influence is immediately rejected by Freud and his disciples. They do not believe in demons and believe little in spiritual things. Yet demonic possession is not only adequately documented in the Bible but is very real in our world today. The counselor may spend a lifetime counseling a demon-possessed person and end up in total frustration and failure. Men and women who are recognized as experts in their field will have no choice but to recommend that the person be locked up because they have no answer. Why? Because the patient is uncontrollable and not sane.

A patient who has a vile temper or uses foul language can erupt at any time. You can be talking to the person, and all of a sudden he opens his mouth and foul language comes out. You say, "How did that happen? What prompted that?" It should be evident to you that a demon is present in that person's life and is arising to direct and control him and to discourage you from further probing. Recognize this behavior for what it is, and don't give in to flaring of tempers and foul speech. The Bible tells us that love never fails. Kind words and a positive manner may cause that possessed person to respond in a positive manner, only to erupt again when you least expect it. This should not be a surprise to you because we see this clearly in the Bible with King Saul.

Let's look at 1 Samuel 19 to see how real this is. As long as David played on the harp, King Saul sat very quietly and was friendly to David. But no sooner had David stopped playing than Saul reached for his javelin to kill David. This is not normal behavior. The Bible says he was driven by an evil spirit. You have to understand the word *driven*. The Bible says "to cast out evil spirits." The King James Version says "to cast out demons." The original text says to "drive" them out. To drive them out means you have to force them out. To force them out, you have to find them. You do not drive rats and mice out of your house until you find them. Then you do something to get rid of them. When you realize demons are present, you have to drive them out. You have to command them, because they do not want to go. Force them!

One Sunday night in our church we saw a demon manifest itself, saying, "I will not leave her! I will not leave her!" The congregation witnessed this. The demon did not want to go. He slammed the woman's body against the floor because he did not want to go. It was not because the woman wanted to hurt herself. When a demon is present and does not want to leave, the person it inhabits becomes a puppet on a string. He will pull the strings, and you will see his physical manifestations. That is why many times you will see a person get so upset. That is not the person; that is not Jesus in the person; that is the demon in the person.

How can Christians be driven by demons? Very simply. They allow themselves to be. The Bible says, "Give [no] place to the devil" (Eph. 4:27). If the Bible says give no place to the devil, it is obvious some Christians give place to the devil. That has been the problem in the body of Christ. Preachers and teachers have not taught the truth. Why? They do not know the truth themselves. How can you teach someone something you do not know or even believe? The Bible says in 1 Samuel 19:9-10, "And the evil spirit from the Lord was upon Saul, as he sat in his house with his javelin in his hand: and David played with his hand. And Saul sought to smite David even to the wall with the javelin; but he slipped away out of Saul's presence, and he smote the javelin into the wall: and David fled, and escaped that night." Now don't tell me Saul was playing games with David. If David had sat there and not moved, the javelin would have gone right through him and nailed him to the wall. The Bible says that while David was playing, Saul sat quietly. As soon as David stopped playing, the evil spirit came back on Saul. Saul wanted to kill David.

Here is what I would like you to see: Jesus encountered people who were demon-possessed. He did not say to them, "Well, let's have a counseling session." When Jesus found people who were demon-possessed, he drove the demons out. He said, "Come out of that man," and the demons departed. Sometimes demons scream. Sometimes they say no. Sometimes they throw the possessed person in the fire. Sometimes the person vomits and foams. We see that when the father brought the boy to Jesus, the disciples could not cast the demon out, but Jesus cast him out. We see all through the Bible how demons have manifested themselves physically.

Those of you who have been in this ministry long enough have seen all kinds of things. You have seen demons operate. A demon may lift a woman three feet off her chair and dump her like a sack of potatoes. That is not natural. That is supernatural.

These things are real, but if you do not understand, how can you solve a problem? How can you help anybody when you have problems yourself? How can you understand how to help a person when you do not understand who is behind the problem? If you understand these things, then the problem is not so big. That is why I tell people who come to me for counseling, "Well, your problem is not big." It isn't, but they have to understand who the problem-causer is. Most people, when you tell them there is demonic activity, will say, "Not me!" Right then I know a demon is there. "Don't tell me I have a demon!" Right there is the evidence, because the voice changes. The person does not realize the demon is speaking through him. I can spot the demons. I can discern who they are. So what did Jesus do? He cast the spirits out; then He counseled the people and said, "Go and sin no more."

We should take the lesson from Jesus. I would not recommend you run out and see if you can find someone who needs a demon cast out. That is not your job. Your job is to be available for Jesus to bring the person to you. You have to know what you are doing (have proper knowledge) before you can do anything. The thing you can do is love the person. The thing you can do is quiet them down. The thing you can do is be gentle. Find out where you can take the person to get help, providing that person needs and wants to be delivered. If he does not want to be delivered and you force him, you will cause problems. You say, "Well, how long do I have to put up with it?" You pray! The Lord knows exactly how to deal with His children. He will help you. He will give you patience, and He will give you understanding in these areas.

In Luke 8:2 we also see that Mary Magdalene had seven devils in her, but once she was delivered she became a follower of Jesus. She became an enthusiastic follower and a true example of Christian character.

I have personally gone through deliverance myself. I have been delivered, and I have prayed for people who have had demons. Some were oppressed, and some were possessed. Using the name of Jesus, demons departed, and the people were set free. Once people have been delivered, as the man at Gadara, they can return home and function as they were created to function. A human being has been created to function in a normal fashion with Christlike character, not with devilish character.

In Luke 8:26-36 we read that the man of Gadara was

demon-possessed. When Jesus got through with him, the Bible says he was "in his right mind" (also in Mark 5:1-15). If he was in his right mind when Jesus got through with him, then he had to be out of his right mind before Jesus got ahold of him. Without such deliverance of demon possession, a person cannot function safely and effectively in society.

Take, for example, a murderer, a Peeping Tom or a rapist. Take any works of the flesh! Galatians 5:16-21 deals with this area. Any person who lives in the works of the flesh is not excluded from demonic attacks. The rapist, the murderer or the Peeping Tom may be in a mental hospital, a jail, a prison or a federal institution. The place does not make any difference. Interview him or counsel with him, and invariably he will say, "I don't know why I did it! I don't know! I don't know what possessed me to do this! That's not me, I'm not like that. I'm normally a nice guy, but something comes over me—something just comes over me—and I'm a different person."

Whenever you cannot control yourself, whether your tongue, your temper, your words or your thought patterns, if you cannot control yourself, it is a demon. God cannot control your tongue. He does not control your thoughts. It is a demon.

Counseling as Sensory Awareness

Most Christians are gullible. Even many of those who go to church do not know the Word. Any Christian, even a babe just born today in the Spirit, knows that wrong is wrong and right is right. The world's attitude is basically "Everybody does it, so let's do it." But when you are born again, you know that attitude is wrong.

In society there are people who are running around claiming to be rehabilitated, but if they are not delivered, they will jump right back into the same situations they were in before. No matter how long they stay in prison, that spirit is still there. It may be dormant, but in the right situation, at the right moment, the trigger will be pulled, and the person falls back into the same destructive behavior pattern.

My heart really goes out to people who try to help others when they themselves do not understand what is happening: even pastors, teachers, the body of Christ. If they do not understand the force behind the trouble, it may look supernatural and therefore attractive. Jesus tells us there is joy for a season in the world, but it is not lasting. We must find a solution that is lasting, and that is to teach people first. Jesus went about teaching, preaching, delivering and healing people.

Recognizing the Transference of Character Traits

The study of transference to the counselor has become one of the most important sources of knowledge pertaining to child psychology. Children are vulnerable. They are very susceptible to whatever happens around them, because spirits will be transferred to them. We study child psychology to observe behavioral change that is taking place, yet we do not know what is causing it. We call these behavioral patterns hereditary, and this is true to a point—a transference has taken place.

When a character trait or behavioral habit of the father or mother begins to show up in a child, a transference has taken place, and that child does not even know it. It seems like overnight these demons begin to activate themselves. They may have been dormant, but they begin to manifest themselves. All of a sudden the child acts awfully.

We have programmed our children to believe that poor behavior is normal, but they do not have to be awful. They do not have to be terrible teenagers. They are beautiful children. God made them. It is difficult to get people even to think in such terms, because the world says "the terrible twos" and "the terrible teenagers." Teenagers are victims of their parents' expectations.

Are they not also victims of, for example, the media, which does

27

nothing but report on the lunatic fringe of the teenage population?

Most Christians would not hold hands with the devil, even if they saw him walking down the street. You would not allow him into your home. You would recognize him as evil, and you would not want to go where he leads. If you are a parent, you would not take your child to a burlesque show. You would not take your child to a sex orgy. You just would not do it, because you know it is not healthy. Yet we allow these same things to come into our homes through television. You would not allow a murderer to come and kill people in your home, yet we allow them to come in through the television. What difference does it make whether the murderer comes through television or through a person or through a newspaper? The spirit does not care. How many Christians do you know who read horoscopes? That's demonic! They live every day to see what so-and-so says is going to happen tomorrow. She or he may be wrong (and most of the time they are wrong), but there is One who can tell you what is going to happen tomorrow, and His name is Jesus. He never misses!

We as Christians must realize that even though television is good, it can be abused and misused. It is our responsibility to control what goes into our home. Even though the world recognizes that transference occurs, people do not know what to call it. They do not know and will not accept that it is a spiritual thing. It is a spiritual phenomenon that takes place in a person's life that they will not admit to. Why? Because they do not understand transference.

I want to point out that there are godly spirits, demonic spirits and human spirits. There is godly wisdom, worldly wisdom and human wisdom. You have to be able to discern and separate all of these. In 1 Corinthians 2:6-8 Paul tells us, "Howbeit we speak wisdom among them that are perfect: yet not the wisdom of this world, nor of the princes of this world, that come to nought: But we speak the wisdom of God in a mystery, even the hidden wisdom, which God ordained before the world unto our glory: [The word *wisdom*, or the *mystery*, is found in 1 Corinthians

4:1-5.] Which none of the princes of this world knew: for had they known it, they would not have crucified the Lord of glory." James 3:13-18 speaks of the wisdom of the world and the wisdom of God.

Now remember the prince of this world. Jesus said in John 14:30, "...for the prince of this world cometh, and hath nothing in me." Jesus could not stop the devil from coming and tempting Him, but He could stop him from getting inside Him. Jesus was saying, in essence, "The devil cannot hold onto anything in Me because I have not given him a place. He cannot use Me. He cannot control Me. He cannot say anything to Me, because I am not his subject. I belong totally to God the Father."

"...They would not have crucified the Lord of glory." Who is the "Lord of glory"? Jesus Christ. Psalm 24 speaks of the "Lord of glory." He is available to all who will make Him Lord of their lives. Look also to see who owns everything: "The earth is the Lord's, and the fulness thereof; the world, and they that dwell therein. [That means the devil is owned by God and is subject to God. God is not subject to the devil.] For he hath founded it upon the seas, and established it upon the floods. Who shall ascend into the hill of the Lord? or who shall stand in his holy place? He that hath clean hands, and a pure heart; who hath not lifted up his soul unto vanity, nor sworn deceitfully. He shall receive the blessing from the Lord, and righteousness from the God of his salvation. This is the generation of them that seek him, that seek thy face, O Jacob. Selah. Lift up your heads, O ye gates; and be ye lift up, ye everlasting doors; and the King of glory shall come in. Who is this King of glory? The Lord strong and mighty, the Lord mighty in battle. Lift up your heads, O ye gates; even lift them up, ye everlasting doors; and the King of glory shall come in. Who is this King of glory? The Lord of hosts, he is the King of glory. Selah" (Psalm 24).

When the Bible says "the Lord of hosts," that means the Lord of war. God says Jesus is the Lord of war. He is the Lord of glory. The Bible is very clear that no matter how big the war is, He is

29

more than enough to win your battle. He is the Lord of glory, but the Bible says they crucified the Lord of glory. Why? Because they didn't know He was the Lord of glory. They thought they were crucifying a man, but He was not just a man. He was God in human flesh.

When Jesus defeated the devil, He did not defeat him as deity. He defeated him as humanity. Glory to God! He did not defeat him as Christ, He defeated him as Jesus. We do not cast demons out in the name of Christ. We cast demons out in the name of Jesus, the human part of Him. I do not know about you, but that is exciting to me! As a human being I can cast the devil out!

Praise God! Hallelujah!

CHAPTER TWO

Good Spirits and Evil Spirits

In our study of transference and counter-transference of spirits, we are going to deal with good spirits and bad spirits. We are also going to deal with human spirits that are influenced by both good and bad spirits, because every human being has a spirit. In addition, we will discuss the difference between transference and influence.

It is important to keep the two separate. Just because you are influenced by a spirit does not mean it has been transferred to you. On the other hand, when a spirit is transferred to you, you have already been influenced by it, whether you know it or not. You made a decision—whether or not you know it is irrelevant to the spirit. So long as there is an open door, the spirit will enter in.

Let me state again, very emphatically, that evil spirits and demons must have a physical body to express themselves; through this body they conduct their activities, habits and behaviors. They cannot do this without a physical body. They prefer human beings, but they will settle for an animal if they have to. In order for them to do the work of their father, the devil, they must have a body.

Jesus, for example, who is the Son of God, came to earth first as a spirit. Then a woman by the name of Mary conceived and gave birth to a child. The Son of God, Jesus, was a spirit before He was born as a child. John 4:24 says, "God is a Spirit." Because God is a Spirit, in order for Him to understand our way of living on this earth, He sent His only begotten Son, and we can prove that scripturally in Hebrews 10:5 and John 1:14.

In Hebrews 10:5 Jesus is speaking: "Wherefore when he cometh into the world..." To find out when He comes into the world, let's go to Matthew 1 where Mary gave birth to Jesus. She did not give birth to Christ. She gave birth to Jesus. This was His human name. His deity name is Christ, the Son of the living God. He says in Hebrews 10:5, "Wherefore when he cometh into the world, he saith..." I like that part. It thrills me that when He came into the world, *He said.* So then we can see that spirits are able to speak apart from the human body. Put yourself in the picture. Let's visualize the birth of Jesus. We know a child that is six hours old does not have the vocabulary to speak, but the Bible says, "Wherefore when he cometh into the world, he saith... " What did He say? To whom was He speaking? He was speaking to the Father. What did He say? "Sacrifice...thou wouldest not, but a body hast thou prepared for me."

God the Father had prepared a woman on the earth, whereby the Spirit of God, our Lord Jesus Christ, could come into the world. So Jesus was able to speak. As soon as He came into the world, He was communicating with His Father. Spirits are able to communicate, with or without the human body.

"Sacrifice...thou wouldest not, but a body hast thou prepared for me." Can you imagine a child six hours old, whether He was in her arms or in a blanket, turning around and saying to Mary, "Sacrifice...thou wouldest not, but a body hast thou prepared for me"? Can you imagine her surprise?

You can see then that it was not his humanity speaking, but rather was deity speaking to deity. This gives us another point on which to meditate. No matter how little the child is, the spirit can communicate to a spirit without the maturity of the flesh. Here Jesus is speaking to the Father just a few seconds after birth into the world.

What does He say in John 1:14? "And the Word was made flesh, and dwelt among us." The Word is Jesus Christ, Son of the living God. The Word became flesh. If the Word became flesh and dwelt among us, it is obvious the Word was not flesh before it dwelt among us. The Word became flesh and tabernacled, or dwelt (lived), among us. The spirit took on a body. For a spirit to dwell on the earth and do what he wants to do, he must have a body. Whether a good spirit or bad spirit, that spirit will dwell in a body.

Jesus dwelt in the body as a good spirit without sin because the nature of Adam was not transferred to Him. Make sure you understand this. The nature of Jesus was from His Father. This is why the Bible doesn't say, "The sins of your mothers will pass on to the generations, to the third and fourth generation." We all have the satanic nature in us, but it is the sins of the fathers that are passed on to the third and fourth generations. The penalty for sin will go on to the third and fourth generations unless we change our nature, unless we recognize the need to change.

Let's review. Transference and counter-transference are real. We see that Reichman and Freud have discovered a certain truth. They were not able to have all the mysteries revealed because they did not have the Bible as a textbook. Their contribution to society has been great, but it was not good enough because they did not recognize the things that the Bible teaches.

The Cause of Unacceptable Behavior

Jesus was not plagued by the things of the world. Society came and tempted Him, but He was never subject to it. Sin did not have dominion over Him. This is not to say that sin was not available to Him—it was—but sin did not have dominion over Him. His nature was different from ours. He was born in the flesh like you and me, but He did not have a bloodline of sin. God does not sin. Jesus' nature was clean. Our nature came from Adam. That is perhaps why we have difficulty with our flesh, because we have been sinners since the day we were born. Jesus was not. Yet He was capable of sin just like you and me; however, He refused to sin.

Sometimes this is difficult for the human mind to grasp. How can a man like Jesus, who was tempted, live without sin, and yet we have difficulty? It is because of our heritage of the satanic nature.

We are dealing with good spirits and bad spirits. Jesus says in Hebrews 10:5, "Wherefore when he cometh into the world, he saith, Sacrifice and offering thou wouldest not, but a body hast thou prepared for me." This was the deity of Jesus speaking. Deity does not have to grow and mature. Deity is already fully grown and fully matured. There is no improvement in deity; He is perfect. Jesus, the Spirit of Christ, was already perfect and mature. He just put on human flesh when He came into the world so He could identify with humanity. So we see that the spirit has to have a body in order to communicate with human beings.

Let me give you several definitions of *transfer*:
1. Transfer means to convey from one person to another, from one place to another or from one situation to another. Hence, spirits can be transferred from one person to another person.
2. Transfer also means an act, or a process—the carry-over of learned responses from one type of situation to another.

Let me give you another illustration of transfer. Transfer is one form of power. Transfer occurs when one form of power is changed into another form of power. For example, a transformer is something that allows power to go through it and be changed. It has the ability. Transference, or transforming, means the changing of power from one to another. That is why when the Word says, "He has delivered us," it means He has transferred us. He delivered us from the power of darkness and translated us into the kingdom of His Son (see Col. 1:13-15).

We see then that transference is used to change one thing to another. It could be good or bad. I am saying all of this because as counselors, as individuals, we have to be careful how we are influenced by surroundings, atmosphere, attitudes, behaviors and spirits. It is up to you to discern the motive of a person, or the spirit in a person. Transference and influence can occur when you are not alert, when you are deceived, even though you are not asking for it.

I will make this point even more clear. I am sure Eve did not ask to be banished from the Garden, but she was influenced, and transfer took place. As a result, she fell for the lesser power and lost her relationship with God. It is an example so you can see how real this is. We will deal with counter-transference later on, but for the time being let me deal with transference of spirits.

The Cause of Unpleasant Hereditary Traits

I am sure you have heard people say, "He's the spitting image of his father," or, "She talks just like her mother," or "He acts just like his father." These are two different human beings, yet they have strong similarities. That could not be genetic because it has nothing to do with their behavior, but heredity could be involved.

Heredity and genetics are two different things. This is what the world falls short of recognizing. *Genetic* is something in your genes such as blue eyes, brown eyes, blond hair, freckled face, etc. All of these things are genetic because they are in the genes. To be loudmouthed and unpleasant in behavior is not genetic. It could be hereditary.

Hereditary spirits may not show up when you are a child, but

35

genetic traits will be there immediately, and you will be able to recognize them. Heredity will creep up when you get older. Then you wonder, "Why am I having the same problems?" or "Why am I doing the same things I saw my mother or father do?"

These are interesting questions! Some of these things may be in your own life. Do not be ashamed of it, but thank God for the revelation and for His grace in showing you these things. With His help you can get rid of them.

To influence means to affect, alter or sway by indirect or intangible means. Influence, then, is power exerted over the mind or behavior of others. Your behavior, or course, involves your will. How many people do you know personally who have influenced you to the point where you begin to act just like they do when you are in their presence? Yet when you are not around them, you act like yourself.

These people, good or bad, are influencing your spirit. The spirit in you, the human spirit, picks up on these behaviors and is activated, whether for good or bad. You start acting like the people around you, and before long you will say, "I don't like the way he acts," or "Seems like every time so-and-so comes around my whole household is in an uproar," or "Every time I get around these people I feel like creepy-crawlies are all over me," or "I get around these people and I just feel so good. It's such a joy to be with them." Do you see how influence works?

It does not mean the spirit has been transferred to you, but it certainly does influence you. Others' power of influence, their activity and their spirit cause you to start behaving as they do. Peer pressure influences young people in this way.

Christians should not be influenced or controlled by the worldly system or spirit. However, in order for you to change, you have to find a different method. The different method, of course, is God's method, and God's method is perfect.

As Christians we should not allow people to make statements

that are contrary to the Word of God. If you feel you might hurt someone's feelings, and so you allow them to say negative statements, that means you are condoning what they say. Because you feel intimidated, you say nothing rather than say something that would stir up conversation you cannot handle. But then you are not correcting the person. In essence, they are influencing you more than you are influencing them, whether it is through your changing their behavior or your not changing their behavior. By not getting involved with them, you are actually involved, and you are being influenced by that.

You say, "How can I even live? I will always have to be on guard." No! When you are full of God's Spirit and know the truth, you will immediately recognize anything that is not the truth. It is not going to register well with your spirit, and you will pick it up immediately. You must be in charge of your spirit and your situation.

I am sure you know people who are successful at influencing others—they are able to sway others. A powerful, radical person who is able to express himself well can affect and sway people his way. On the other hand, a person who is radically against the devil and has a good spirit also has the power and ability to affect and sway people. We can look to Jesus for our example.

Whenever Jesus appeared, He influenced people. He affected their lives. We see people in the world today who use this influence. In order to influence anyone, you have to have power behind you. Without power it cannot be done.

The origin of occult power—"the act or power of producing an effect without apparent exertion of force"—has been said to be derived from the stars. It has also been said that celestial, heavenly, unworldly, spiritual, immaterial, intangible fluid flows from the stars to affect the actions of men. This is what the world would like us to believe. The world wants us to think that such is the source of their occult power.

The spirits are after your mind. Wherever their power emanates from, God or the devil, they are concerned with your mind. We know that God does not control the minds of His people. However, we have to understand our minds in order to make a decision. Most of the time the devil will force you to think in these terms. In order for him to do this, he first has to have an entry point.

The following is what is said about psychotherapy sessions according to Freud and many others: "The therapist attempts to respond to the patient in a highly dynamic interaction and interpersonal communication." They are able to communicate. "…Through highly dynamic interaction and interpersonal communication, transference and counter-transference may occur." This is where the terminology comes from.

When a therapist, psychotherapist or counselor begins to communicate with an individual, transference and counter-transference may occur, and many times they do occur. This is not healthy.

How do we deal with this? You have no doubt been with people who have taken on everybody else's problems. Rest assured that counter-transference has occurred. As a counselor, when you walk around with someone else's problems, you have become a victim of counter-transference of those problems. Jesus says, "Put all your burdens on Me, because I care for you" (see 1 Pet. 5:7). If Jesus says, "Put all your burdens on Me," but *you* take them on, in essence you have replaced Jesus, and you are now teaching a theory of Freud and Reichman rather than the Word of God.

This is crucial. When you counsel people, you must not allow their problems to become your problems. I have not only found this among counselors but among intercessors. Intercessors are known for counter-transference of spirits. Intercessors are known to walk around with problems. Intercessors are known to walk around with long faces. You will find that most intercessors who desire to pray for others do not know how to protect themselves. As a result, the devil comes in and starts condemning them, criticizing them and causing their flesh to rule them.

CHAPTER THREE

Unto the Third and Fourth Generation

L et's look at how real transference and counter-transference of spirits is. Exodus 20:1-5 says, "And God spake all these words, saying, I am the Lord thy God, which have brought thee out of the land of Egypt, out of the house of bondage. Thou shalt have no other gods before me. Thou shalt not make unto thee any graven image, or any likeness of any thing that is in heaven above, or that is in the earth beneath, or that is in the water under the earth: Thou shalt not bow down thyself to them, nor serve them: for I the Lord thy God am a jealous God, visiting the iniquity of the fathers upon the children unto the third and fourth generation of them that hate me."

Fathers who sin produce children who sin. The iniquities of the fathers are passed on to their children. God did not ordain it to be so. God says you can prevent this by not serving other gods and by serving the Lord God Almighty. Those who have chosen to serve other gods have put something else in place of God. "And shewing mercy unto thousands of them that love me, and keep my commandments" (Ex. 20:6). Here is a clear-cut picture of how we can stop the iniquities of the fathers from flowing to our generation. If we love Him and follow Him, He will show us mercies.

In Exodus 34:7 basically the same passage is given. "Keeping mercy for thousands, forgiving iniquity and transgression and sin, and that will by no means clear the guilty; visiting the iniquity of the fathers upon the children, and upon the children's children, unto the third and to the fourth generation." So it is clear then that spirits are passed from the fathers to their children and their children's children. There is definitely a transference, a follow-up or a progression that takes place. As fathers and parents we have a tremendous responsibility for our children.

Numbers 14:18 says, "The Lord is longsuffering, and of great mercy, forgiving iniquity and transgression, and by no means clearing the guilty, visiting the iniquity of the fathers upon the children unto the third and fourth generation." God is a very consistent God. He says, "If you do what I ask you to do, you will be pardoned. If you do not do what I ask you to do, you will be punished. You will receive the reward of the seed that you sow."

Numbers 14:23 talks about the children of Israel who rebelled against God: "Surely they shall not see the land which I sware unto their fathers, neither shall any of them that provoked me see it." Their fathers had sinned, and because their fathers had sinned, they would not see the land or the promises that God had given to their fathers.

Now let's see what verse 24 says: "But my servant Caleb, because he had another spirit with him, and hath followed me fully, him will I bring into the land whereinto he went; and his seed shall possess it." When He says "because he has another spirit," it tells me that Caleb and Joshua chose to serve the Spirit of God. Because they obeyed the Spirit of God, that Spirit was passed on from them to their seed, and they were able to possess the promises of God. Those fathers who rejected the Spirit of God and took on a spirit contrary to the Spirit of God did not inherit the promises of God. We see a consistency in this.

Deuteronomy 5:6-10 says, "I am the Lord thy God, which brought thee out of the land of Egypt, from the house of bondage. Thou shalt have none other gods before me. Thou shalt not make thee any graven image, or any likeness of any thing that is in heaven above, or that is in the earth beneath, or that is in the waters beneath the earth: Thou shalt not bow down thyself unto them, nor serve them: for I the Lord thy God am a jealous God, visiting the iniquity of the fathers upon the children unto the third and fourth generation of them that hate me, and shewing mercy unto thousands of them that love me and keep my commandments." The same thing He repeats again. When God takes time to repeat His message a second time, it would behoove us to pay attention. God does not say things lightly. He says what He says because He means it. This emphasis on the underlying statement indicates that God wants us to serve Him and His Spirit.

First Peter 5:5-7 says, "Likewise, ye younger, submit yourselves unto the elder. Yea, all of you be subject one to another, and be clothed with humility: for God resisteth the proud, and giveth grace to the humble. Humble yourselves therefore under the mighty hand of God, that he may exalt you in due time. *Casting all* your care upon him, for he careth for you" (italics added). That is the key verse. "Casting all your care upon him, for he careth for you."

In my opinion the psychological cannot be properly understood without the spiritual; neither can it be divorced from it. You cannot separate the soul from the spirit. They are so closely knit together that you cannot say, "We will take the soul of a man and neglect the spirit. We will deal with the mind and not the spirit." The only place I can find a line of demarcation between the soul and the spirit is in the Word of God. No man-made instrument can find the line of separation between the soul and spirit. Yet secular experts have taken upon themselves to say, "We do not believe in the

41

spirit. We only believe in the soul. We give all of the attention to the soul and not the spirit." They neglect one-third of a person. The most important part is the spirit. I want to be very emphatic and go on record as saying I believe the only thing that can truly separate the soul from the spirit is the Word of God. God made the soul and the spirit.

To prove my point scripturally, look at Hebrews 4:12. "For the word of God is quick, and powerful, and sharper than any two-edged sword, piercing even to the dividing asunder of soul and spirit,... [We can see then that the soul and the spirit are two separate entities. The only thing powerful enough to separate them is the Word of God.] ...and of the joints and marrow, and is a discerner of the thoughts and intents of the heart."

Who Is Responsible for Your Behavior?

Psychiatrists and psychologists and those who classify themselves as experts in these fields acknowledge the fact that we do have bones, marrow, a brain and the ability to think and reason. They have done a great deal of research to find this out. What they do not acknowledge is that man is influenced by a power source, either good or evil. We have the ability to think and make decisions, but there is a force behind this ability. I cannot stress how important it is for you, as a Christian, to realize we are being influenced by these forces. We must know who they are. My purpose in publishing this material is to illustrate the difference between influence and transference of spirits.

Behavior brought about by influence can be changed or corrected, but you cannot change a spirit. A spirit has to be cast out. Let me show you what I mean by this. If I am in your presence and I do not like what you are saying, I can change that influence by leaving the room and not associating with you. As another example, if the sun is shining outside, I can be influenced by the sunshine to leave my house and go outside. It could pull me in that direction. Influence pulls you towards something or away from something else. With transference something enters in. There is a

42

difference. You can change influence by removing yourself from the situation. You can change facts. For instance, if you live up north where there are cold winters, you can change that fact of your life by moving where there is no snow. Facts can be changed, but a transference of spirits you cannot change. If you are tormented by the devil up north and think that by going to Florida you will get rid of your problems, you will find that the problems intensify. You cannot run away from a spirit. You have to deal with the spirit by recognizing and renouncing it. Deliverance is essential, even for Christians. If you do not recognize the spirit, it will be very difficult for you to deal with the situation.

It is interesting to note that the specialists who are probing into the psychological part of man use terminology such as transference and counter-transference. They are aware that something is happening, but they do not have the answer. They are worried. They know a change takes place. Let me tell you about change and influence with possession of a seventeen-year-old man. He was involved in satanic worship. He killed his own father and mother and used blood to make a covenant with Satan. He sold his soul to the devil, writing with his own blood on a piece of paper to have supernatural power. People say, "Well, that's not real." I have the article.

Let me give you several names so you can see how close to the truth these people are, and yet how far away they are: David W. Shave is a medical doctor. From his writing we gather that transference is a phenomenon based on a primary process that he calls *para-pro-toto*. Para-pro-toto is where the therapist is viewed unconsciously by the patient as someone with whom he was emotionally involved in the past. It is therefore not just reliving the past but an evidence of repressed hostility of infantile objects. Shave has found that as you counsel a person, that person views you as the person of the past, good or bad, and is able to bring forth the hostility that came into them as a child. As an adult this hostility has caused the patient psychological problems. In viewing the counselor as a para-pro-toto, the hostility is transferred to the subject of the infantile stage of that person. With this hostility transferred to the counselor, the counselor now becomes the carrier. There is danger in that.

What Shave has found is true to some degree. The counselor is able to bring out the hurt of the past. However, if the counselor does not realize he is not God and does not know that the past is to be transferred to Jesus and does not prepare the counselee beforehand, he opens himself up. When you counsel people, spirits could very easily transfer to you. However, if you are aware of this and know that you are not God, you will not take what the counselee dishes out. You will give it to the Lord Jesus. Prepare your patient and tell him this is what the Lord says. This is what experts say they have discovered, but they have not discovered that there is a way out. In that case both the patient and the counselor are in the same boat, and that boat sinks rapidly. You can see why the world has so many problems.

Are You a Prisoner of Someone Else's Habits?

Psychologically immature patients with severe dependency needs may transfer these needs to the therapist. The therapist, sensing the psychopathological emotional state of the individual, allows the patient to draw support and strength. As the therapist responds, counter-transference occurs. The danger lies in the possibility of traumatic interpersonal relationships developing as a result. In other words, then they both are dealing with a spirit.

Suppose I am carrying on a conversation with you, and you lash out at me in anger. If I do not stop it right then and act in love, or perhaps walk away, but instead respond to the comment just thrown at me, am I receiving your anger?

In order for the anger to become a part of you, you must come into agreement with it. When you come into agreement with it, you open yourself up. But let's not get spooked and say, "I'm not going to counsel anybody because a spirit is going to jump on me." It cannot jump on you unless you take part, start sympathizing with that spirit, agreeing with it. Only then will it draw you in. It is a matter of receiving it. Of course, there is no intention that such a relationship should develop, according to another expert named Reusch.

Reusch says that the initial phase of therapy is devoted to getting acquainted and discovering the patient's methods of communication. The therapist listens, giving the patient an opportunity to speak, perhaps adding a word to assist the patient in communicating, but he waits for the transference of neurosis to develop. He waits for the patient to open up. The patient must open up in order for the therapist to begin analysis. The counselor has to win the confidence of the counselee. The patient desperately wants someone to listen to him and offer answers to his questions. Reusch's point of view is this: When you counsel a person, listen to what he has to say. As you win his confidence, he will open up and share with you so that you can share with him, establishing communication.

For anything to be resolved, there has to be open communication. But in the unloading of the patient's problems onto the counselor, it is important that the counselor not become a container, or receiver, of those problems.

Reichman emphasizes that the approach to neurotic or psychotic patients is to delve into and discover the trauma and damage done in their interpersonal childhood relationships. These defects are considered primal in later development in some psychopathological situations. Such therapeutic probings lend themselves to dependencies on transferences and counter-transferences. To paraphrase, those people who rely on you as their source or crutch will never grow up. They will always lean on you and always come to you. They will never become mature. That dependence in childhood that influences them will always cause them to depend on you. They will be very insecure in society.

Most psychiatrists will agree that the treatment of the emotionally ill is dependent upon the basic emotional involvement of the therapist. They know it is important for the therapist to truly

45

empathize with the patient, to feel what the patient is experiencing, in order for successful counseling to take place.

Shave wrote that a therapist who takes on a real problem of the patient introduces into therapy a serious patient vector. *Vector* is derived from the word *vectus*, which means "carrier." Shave says that in order for both therapist and patient to be effective in their relationship, the therapist must take on a real problem of the patient and become the patient vector, or carrier, which is totally opposite from God's Word.

I am giving you these examples so you can understand where the world of psychoanalysis is coming from. This is why so many people in the world are not being helped. The Bible says the blind lead the blind. When the blind lead the blind, both will get hurt. Most of the time this is what happens. Again, let me make a reference to 1 Peter 5:5-8. The Bible says we have to put *all* of our cares on the Lord Jesus Christ.

Shave describes counter-transference as the therapist's biggest asset in dealing with a troubled patient. If that person is demon-controlled or demon-possessed, think what would happen to a therapist or counselor if he opened himself up for counter-transference of the spirits.

The point I am making here is that modern psychiatry calls this a transference. They do not say it is a transference of a human spirit, a spirit of God or an evil spirit. They simply recognize the transference and hope it is a mutually beneficial transfer between patient and therapist. They hope that by allowing themselves to be the "sponge," the patient is relieved of his problems. But where are the problems going? We must understand we are dealing with a spirit. It is like taking a pitcher of water and pouring the water into a glass. The water does not disappear but is merely moved from one vessel to another.

If transference is to be understood we must understand mankind and the communication process from multidimensional viewpoints, not just from the standpoint of mind and body. There are other sources we must understand. Man has delved into the practices of hypnosis and occult communication—thus, into the spirit world. Why? Because man always seeks the supernatural. God made him so.

Parapsychology is nothing but clairvoyance. *Psychokinesis* means the moving of physical objects by the mind without the use of physical means. Psychokinesis is real. It has surfaced with wide acceptance, even to the point that Christians are interested in finding out more about it.

A man can do all that he can and study all that he wants to study, but he will never come to knowledge of the truth unless he accepts Jesus Christ as his Savior. Jesus said, "I am...the truth" (John 14:6). The only way to find out about supernatural things is to have a supernatural God in you. Christians have no business inquiring into clairvoyance and psychokinesis. It is real, but it is not for us.

When Freud first projected the phenomenon of transference, it was rejected by most. He believed the decisive battle for recapturing a patient's mental health was to concentrate all of the patient's biological urges, libido, desires and lusts in a transference, thus freeing him of all infantile conflicts. Can you beat that? Freeing them of all their infantile conflicts by transference of these infantile problems to the analyst. Although his teaching was rejected at first, it is widely accepted today. The question I have is, What will the therapist do with these problems? Where does it leave him? This harks back to humanism—that we as individuals are our own gods and do not need God.

The libidinal process, or concept, was simply to find in the analyst a father or mother or other person who would give the patient what the original parent did not give him, either positive or negative. Under this process, the analyst becomes a dumping ground. He puts himself in a very dangerous situation.

As a Christian counselor, you are there to discern and teach the person and show him the answer to his problem. The answer is Jesus. He is the One who can solve the problems. You are there as a representative of Jesus to show the patient that, yes, this is a problem, but here is how we can solve it. You do not become God, but you become God's representative. You do not take on the problems of every person. When people come to my office, I know what spirits are operating, and I am able to give all the cares unto the Lord. I am always going to God and asking Him for wisdom and direction. I cannot deal with these spirits in my own strength, but because of God I can and do deal with them.

The therapist, by the process of repetition, must extract the hate neurosis of the patient. He goes over it and gets the person to open up. This obligates the therapist not only to interpret, but also to teach, guide, educate, prohibit and demand. He becomes the authoritarian.

When I become the authoritarian in the counseling situation and say, "You can't do this," rebellion arises within you, the counselee. If, for example, your father was very authoritarian, this may rouse you to anger. You are angry at me because I remind you of your father, so naturally the anger is stirred up. I stirred up that spirit within you. The anger is now going to come at me. That puts me in a dangerous situation. If I do not know how to protect myself, I could be controlled by that spirit as well.

What the therapist tries to do, of course, is split the personality of the patient. When a person has multiple personalities and a counselor tries to split these personalities and deal with each of them, my question is, "Who are these personalities? Where are they coming from?" As an individual, how can you have multiple personalities? The clinical term for this is *schizophrenia*.

Schizophrenia is a compound word. In Greek *schizo* means "to split." *Phrenia* means "personality," or "frantic." The word *frantic* means "mind disorder." Phrenia of that personality is a mind disorder or withdrawal from reality into fantasy or delusion. Hence, schizo is a split personality; phrenia, or frantic, is a mind disorder or withdrawal from reality into fantasy or delusion. If you have a split personality, that means you have more than one. If you have more than one, who put them there? Who are they? Where are they from? All of these different personalities have different behaviors. Question: Is God confused? No! Does God have split personalities? No! It is obvious, then, that these do not come from God. Yet a person is capable of being in this condition.

Does the split personality of the schizophrenic make him frantic? Definitely. Confusion takes place. That is why people say, "I just don't know what to do with myself." Why don't they know what to do? Because the personalities are taking over. That is why a young man can say, "I don't remember killing my mother. I don't remember killing my father. I don't remember any of that."

Counseling as Effective Release

The role of a psychiatrist is indeed a difficult one. Very few understand or would agree that probing through hypnosis is another form of seance. Many Christians submit themselves to hypnosis. It is another form of seance and communication with latent spirits of hatred, lust, bitterness and even suicidal spirits.

For example, a psychiatrist counsels a rapist or someone guilty of incest or murder and pronounces them temporarily insane. You read this every day. After several sessions over a period of months, they are released as cured and fit to live in society. Temporarily insane people who are "rehabilitated" are only temporarily subdued. King Saul is a good example of this. They soon react to internal driving forces. You do not cure a drug addict by taking him away from drugs and locking him up. You do not cure a murderer by putting him in jail for twenty or thirty years and trying to rehabilitate him. We are not dealing with the person; we are dealing with the spirit in the person.

In 1 Samuel 16:13-23 it says, "Then Samuel took the horn of oil, and anointed him in the midst of his brethren: and the spirit of the Lord came upon David from that day forward. So Samuel rose up, and went to Ramah. But the spirit of the Lord departed from Saul, and an evil spirit from the Lord troubled him. And Saul's servants said unto him, Behold now, an evil spirit from God troubleth thee. Let our lord now command thy servants, which are before thee, to seek out a man, who is a cunning player on an harp: and it shall come to pass, when the evil spirit from God is upon thee, that he shall play with his hand, and thou shalt be well. And Saul said unto his servants, Provide me now a man that can play well, and bring him to me. Then answered one of the servants, and said, Behold, I have seen a son of Jesse the Bethlehemite, that is cunning in playing, and a mighty valiant man, and a man of war, and prudent in matters, and a comely person, and the Lord is with him. Wherefore Saul sent messengers unto Jesse, and said, Send me David thy son, which is with the sheep. And Jesse took an ass laden with bread, and a bottle of wine, and a kid, and sent them by David his son unto Saul. And David came to Saul, and stood before him: and he loved him greatly; and he became his armourbearer. And Saul sent to Jesse, saying, Let David, I pray thee, stand before me; for he hath found favour in my sight. And it came to pass, when the evil spirit from God was upon Saul, that David took an harp, and played with his hand: so Saul was refreshed, and was well, and the evil spirit departed from him."

The biblical text says the spirit is from God: "Let our lord now command thy servants, which are before thee, to seek out a man, who is a cunning player on an harp: and it shall come to pass, when the evil spirit from God is upon thee, that he shall play with his hand, and thou shalt be well. And Saul said unto his servants, Provide me now a man that can play well, and bring him to me" (vv. 16-17).

When David played, the spirit departed. Here is what I want you to understand: God did not have an evil spirit. Saul had an evil spirit. God is the One who tells the evil spirit to come or not to come. God can stop an evil spirit. It was not that God put an evil spirit on Saul. No. God cannot sin. God does not tempt anyone. God cannot have an evil spirit; however, God permits all things. In this respect God will not stop an evil spirit from coming upon you if you do wrong. Saul did wrong. Because he sinned, he opened himself up to allow the evil spirit. When the sons of God came to see God in Job 1, Satan also came before God. God said, "What are you doing here?" Satan replied, "I've been running to and fro in the earth, and I have no one to torment." God said, "Have you considered My servant Job? He is perfect." Satan said, "Yes, but You have a hedge around him. I can't touch him." God said, "See, he is yours." The Bible says that Satan departed from the presence of God and went to torment Job, but the Bible also records that God said to the devil, "But don't touch his soul." The evil spirits were able to afflict Job because he had already torn the hedge. The devil had every right to enter and torment him. When a person is not right with God, then evil spirits have a right to enter into that person and torment him. God did not send the evil spirit; He permitted it.

The law says, "Thou shalt not serve any other gods." If you do, God cannot stop the devil from coming and tempting you. He has given you the power to stop him from coming in, but if you do not stop him, you open yourself to evil spirits. The devil is not in charge. God is in charge. Saul invited the spirit to come in through his evil deeds of anger, rage and murder. As soon as the evil spirit departed, Saul received peace. But when David stopped playing the harp, the evil spirit came back on Saul, who picked up his javelin and tried to kill David.

Spirits are able to enter and depart. It depends on what kind of life you live as to what kind of spirits will be there. You may have a preacher who is on fire for God and doing well today, but what is he like tomorrow? If you go based on what he was like yesterday and sit under his teaching, you could be in trouble. You could have a seducing spirit attack you. That is why the Bible says to test the spirits.

A man who is born again and filled with the Spirit of God knows that greater is He that is within him than he that is within the world. You do not have to be afraid of the spirits attacking you when you live a godly life. Most of you recognize when someone

51

says things that cause you to feel like a big ball just dropped in the pit of your stomach, and you don't bear witness to it. You know it is wrong. You do not know it intellectually. You may not even have a scripture for it, but on the inside you know. That is your spirit saying it is not right. If you disobey that still small voice within you and do your own thing, you open yourself up, and transference and counter-transference could easily take place. You will need deliverance.

Because of ignorance of the Word, you will sometimes say, "Well, this person is a Christian." But the more of God's Word you have, the more revelation you will have, the more knowledge you will have and the cleaner you will be. As a matter of fact, when you are full of God's Word you will be able to discern the spirits everywhere you go. However, if you open yourself to those spirits, you will need deliverance. That does not mean you are not going to heaven. It does mean you have problems.

CHAPTER FOUR

Demon Possession and Oppression

My great concern is that counselors understand spiritual forces. As mentioned previously, if a therapist is dealing with a demon-possessed person, but he himself does not understand or even recognize the reality of the spirit world, how can he help that person? He cannot! He may pacify the person for the time being, and it is scriptural to suppress a spirit with kind and gentle words, but that spirit will manifest itself later in life.

If the patient is demon-oppressed or demon-possessed and does not receive deliverance, he cannot effectively or safely function in society. He is a prisoner within himself. How many people do you know personally who are prisoners within themselves because they do not have freedom? For instance, the rapist, child molester, murderer or anyone living in the works of the flesh (see Gal. 5:19-21) lives every day to commit those acts to which they are inclined. Is that the nature of a human being? No! Anyone who kills another person, when they come to their right mind through remorse, will feel bad about what they have done. As you interview the patient or counsel with him, invariably he will say, "I don't know why I did it. I really didn't mean to do that. Something just came over me. I couldn't control myself. I just don't know why I did it. That's not me."

This person is crying out to you. He is saying, "I have this problem. I don't know how to deal with it. I'm looking for help." The woman in Acts 16 came and testified of Paul and Silas, "These are the men of God preaching the gospel." She was controlled by a spirit of divination within her, a familiar spirit. She was crying, "They are bringing salvation to us." She was crying for deliverance. Thank God that Paul was sensitive enough to the spirit world to recognize the demon and cast it out of her, setting her free. Religious men were using her for their own selfish gain. Religious men and women today will still use others for their own selfish gain. Religious spirits can gain access to people, and they do not care what happens so long as they get their own needs met.

Who Is Controlling You?

When a person says, "I don't know why I did it. I didn't want to do it," he is telling you he is a prisoner within himself. He wants someone to set him free. Be sensitive and perceptive in your response. Don't just say, "You have a demon in you." That is not going to get the person to open up. He may not even know what you are talking about. He may not even believe in demons. Instead, approach him in such a way as to help him open up. You have to perform a spiritual operation. Having performed the spiritual operation, you must also "sew him up properly" or the operation fails.

Let's use an illustration. Take a hospital operating room. A surgeon goes in and prepares for surgery. The nurses scrub the patient. They dress him for the operation, and everything else is readied for the procedure. The operation is carried out perfectly. Everything is fine up to this point. But suppose the surgeon says, "I am through with the patient. I have cut out the problem, and now the patient is going to live." They put the patient on a stretcher and take him, without sewing him up, outside in the broiling sun and leave him there. Was the operation successful? The operation is not successful until the patient has recovered. You may do the cutting, and you may even extract the problem, but if you do not take time to sew up the patient, you have only done half of the operation. You did not complete the operation, and the patient dies because you did not follow through. A good physician sees to it that the person is sewn up and visits him daily to make sure that all systems are improving. If they are not improving, something is wrong. You must then search out the cause of the problem.

Physical operations are no different from spiritual operations. You may not realize what you are doing, but the Bible says the Word of God is sharper than any two-edged sword. It is sharper than the physician's scalpel. In essence, you are using the Word of God to perform a spiritual operation. If you do only half the operation by putting the patient out in the sun without sewing him up and giving him proper medication, that patient could well die because of your negligence.

It is important for you to schedule times with those whom you are counseling where you will be responsible for their well-being until they are healthy and doing well. It is your responsibility. Realize that when a person says, "Something came over me, and I couldn't help it," they are saying, "Someone else is controlling me. I am a prisoner, and they use me at will." If they are used at will, who is using them? I don't control you. God does not control the hearts and minds of His people. Who is it then? You don't have to be too smart to figure it out, but you could be religious and deny the fact that a Christian can be tormented by demons. Demons get in through ignorance or through sin.

I want to drive this point home. When you are a counselor or therapist, you may sit by the hour with such a person. His behavior seems normal. He seems congenial and even repentant about his sin. He promises he will never do it again. "I have learned my lesson," he says. "That is the last time." The therapist, not recognizing that demons are real and present, though latent or dormant, pronounces the patient rehabilitated and ready to resume normal life because he acts normal. Then, to the therapist's surprise and amazement, the patient falls into the same state and/or behaviors as before, and he does not understand what went wrong.

Think of all the prisons and mental hospitals where the devil has God's people locked up simply because we do not know how to cope with their problems. I have seen people who have gone to jail and spent years there, even taking religion as their profession. They came out ordained men of the cloth wearing their black robes and white collars, supposedly reformed and carrying around huge Bibles. For the first two weeks they were sincere. I soon found out that one of them became the biggest drug pusher in town.

A person may take part in religious activities and be ordained by certain denominations, but if he is not delivered from tormenting spirits, he can revert back to his former state. How? By returning to old habits and environments. It does not matter who you are. You may be a minister and turn around and sin like everyone else.

Demons can lie dormant for a long time. That is why you may not find this behavior in people until the right situation presents itself. Deliverance, according to the Word of God, is the way to set captives free.

My heart goes out to those who sincerely try to help. As therapists or counselors, they desire to help suffering humanity. They may become dangerously involved in transference and counter-transference, not realizing that so often they are involved in the occult and the problem itself. That's why you find that so many psychiatrists and psychologists who are not born again have so many problems in their own lives. It is sad to see. And yet psychiatry recognizes that if I, as a therapist, spend enough time with a patient, that patient will pull me in. That is the hazard of the profession. It does not have to be so.

How to Be Free from the Control of Others

Therapists or counselors should inquire into the possibility of the patient being possessed or oppressed by a demon rather than just labeling the problem as infantile neurosis. The therapist says, "That child was apparently abused or misused, and now anger, frustration, certain sexual drives and alcoholism are manifesting in him." They call it infantile neurosis. It is demonic oppression. It is a spiritual problem that must be dealt with on a spiritual level. It must be done or the person will always have problems.

If such is the case, deliverance or healing can only be effected through the biblical provision of deliverance.

In presenting deliverance to a person, take time to teach him spiritual truths. I would not recommend you do otherwise unless it is an emergency situation and you must deal with it. In that case you must go ahead with deliverance, but I would strongly recommend you take time to reach such a person, advise him and relate to him using parables of Jesus. Jesus taught using parables. Spiritual things have to be brought down to the natural level where a person can grasp their meaning. Normally people do not have a point of reference on a spiritual level. Parables teach spiritual truths through the use of everyday examples.

Galatians 5:19-21 says, "Now the works of the flesh are manifest, which are these; Adultery, fornication, uncleanness, lasciviousness, idolatry, witchcraft, hatred, variance, emulations, wrath, strife, seditions, heresies, envyings, murders, drunkenness, revellings, and such like: of the which I tell you before, as I have also told you in time past, that they which do such things shall not inherit the kingdom of God."

Murder and strife are listed in the same category as envy. Do not have the attitude, "Oh, he's a murderer, so he's not going to go to heaven." What about your heart? What about strife? What about envying? What about bickering? What about all of these other things?

A drunkard is one who drinks all the time. Paul did not say you could not have a glass of wine. He did not say you are not going to be angry at times. He did not say that if you utter a negative word you will not inherit the kingdom of God. He is saying, "If you practice these things..." A gossiper is one who gossips all the time. If you practice the works of the flesh you are not willing to obey the Word. You are going to do whatever you want to do. But God says, "If you listen to Me and you are willing to be corrected, your sins (the works of the flesh) will be forgiven."

The key here is practicing. In other words, anything you do habitually, not being willing to be corrected, indicates you do not have a teachable spirit. The Bible says you are then willingly turning yourself over to that area. The Bible says that you are not going to take it to heaven with you. I did not write the Bible, and I am not the judge. I am just telling you to read what is there so you will be able to bring people to the Word in counseling. They will have to make a choice. When you bring a person to the Word, then you are out of the picture. The blame is not going to be on you.

The Word will do one of two things—drive you closer to God or drive you away from God. Those who are willing to follow the Lord and do right have a teachable spirit. Those who do not will find an excuse as to why they should not.

We just read in the Bible that these works of the flesh are of demonic origin. Therapists may call them infantile hang-ups, neuroses or images. Clergymen in the past have also not recognized these behaviors for what they are, but thank God they are now discovering there is a total cure for such after regeneration and deliverance. They are realizing that a person can be set free.

When people came to Jesus, He healed them all and cast out demons. All kinds of people were brought to Jesus. Jesus did not force them. They came to Him. There will be times when people will call you and say, "Go and pray for so-and-so." So-and-so may not want you to come and pray for them. If so-and-so wants you to pray for them, let so-and-so get in touch with you and say, "I need help." Then ask the Lord if you should go. If the Lord says not to go, don't go. Do not be a puppet for everyone to pull your strings, because they will wear you out. When you start counseling people, do not counsel at home. Do not give your phone number to the counselees. This is Rule Number One. It is not being cruel. It is being wise. Jesus did not have everybody come to His home. He went where they were, and then they came to Him from the crowds. He healed them and cast demons out of them. If it worked for Jesus, I am confident it will work for us too.

The Bible says in Matthew 4:24 that they came to Him and He healed them all. If He healed them all, then, praise God, there is something for us to consider. I would suggest that you and I not be like the Pharisees, Sadducees and many clergy of the day. We should not try to improve upon God's methods. If He says, "Heal the sick," then heal the sick. If He says, "Cast out demons," then cast out demons. Do not say, "It is not for today." The Bible is for today. Jesus is for today. The power of God is for today. The devil is still at large, and we have power in Jesus' name to cast him out.

Note that in the story in Mark 5 the man was emotionally and mentally deranged and beset by demons. Why is it so difficult for us today to find the same answer for people who have these problems?

Mark 5:1-6 says, "And they came over unto the other side of the sea, into the country of the Gadarenes. And when he was come out of the ship, immediately there met him out of the tombs a man with an unclean spirit, who had his dwelling among the tombs; and no man could bind him, no, not with chains. Because that he had been often bound with fetters and chains, and the chains had been plucked asunder by him, and the fetters broken in pieces: neither could any man tame him. And always, night and day, he was in the mountains, and in the tombs, crying, and cutting himself with stones. But when he saw Jesus afar off, he ran and worshipped him."

My friend, as soon as you get over one particular situation

another arises. Read chapter 4 and you will see that just as Jesus got over this situation, another one arose. The devil is not going to leave you alone when you win one battle. He is going to present another battle. He is waiting to see what you are going to do. Learn a lesson from Jesus about how He handled this particular battle. And be aware that as long as you have Jesus on the inside, the devil will always try to confront you and steal away the power God has given you.

The Gadarene man was trying to help himself, and on the inside he was crying out, but no one would help him. Men put fetters on him and threw him out. He was not allowed to dwell among people. He lived among the tombs and mountains. He cried out and tore those chains off. When he saw Jesus, the Bible says he ran and worshipped Him.

This was a possessed man who yet had a mentality to think logically. When he saw Jesus, he saw the answer. He ran to the answer. Even this man desired to be free. Perhaps he thought to himself that Jesus heard his cry. In essence his cry was his prayer. The Bible says when this man saw Jesus, he ran to Him and worshipped Him. No matter how much the devil controls a person, deep inside that individual is crying out for help. The Bible says, "Call unto me, and I will answer thee, and shew thee great and mighty things, which thou knowest not" (Jer. 33:3). Man could not help him. Psychiatrists could not help him. Doctors could not help him. But Jesus came on the scene, and there came the answer. Because the man cried out, Jesus took time to answer.

That scripture gives a true example of seeing a person in the spirit rather than in the natural. No wonder no one could help the demoniac. Everybody looked at him the way he was and dealt with him from a natural perspective. Jesus, seeing the man, saw the spirit that indwelt the man. When he cried out with a loud voice, saying, "What have I to do with thee, Jesus, thou Son of the most high God? I adjure thee by God, that thou torment me not" (Mark 5:7), that was the spirit speaking. Jesus said, "Come out of the man, thou unclean spirit" (v. 8). He was recognizing the spirit rather than the outward man.

With supernatural problems, man is not able to help another using natural means. Jesus, being a man, understood the needs of men and had understanding of the supernatural as well. No matter how good a man may be as a doctor, psychiatrist or psychologist, if he does not understand the supernatural—the spiritual torment of the patient—he cannot help the person. Jesus made Himself available because there was a need. The man ran to Him.

The devil recognized Jesus. The demon recognized Jesus. It was the man that ran to Jesus. The demon didn't run to Jesus. The man had a will even though he was demon-possessed. He was not taught by Jesus, and he was not taught in the synagogues that there was a Messiah coming. The Bible does not tell us that. The man had been possessed by demon spirits.

If some psychiatrists believe that transference and counter-transference can take place between a patient and therapist, why is it so difficult for so many Christians to believe that anger, jealousy, backbiting, hatred, strife, vexation and all of such that the Bible calls spirits can be transferred from one person to another? Not only from unsaved individuals who have anger but individuals who claim to be men and women of God who have these behaviors. If you associate with such people, what would prevent a spirit from getting you if you do not protect yourself? Psychiatrists acknowledge this. Yet Christians say, "Oh, I don't believe that can happen. I'm a born-again Christian." Your spirit is born again but your flesh is not. You still have the same dirty, unredeemed flesh that you had when you were a sinner. The Bible tells us this in Romans 8:23. We are still waiting for the redemption of our bodies. We have been born again. We have been washed by the blood against the inward sin of our spirit. Our spirit is born again, and our soul is saved. But our soul has to be washed daily by the Word. The flesh will start looking better, smelling better and feeling better. Why? Because the man who dwells on the inside takes care of his house.

You do not have to go too far to see the difference. You can go from one side of town to the other and see it. One area is nice and clean because people take care of it, but the other is all broken down. We call these slums. Why? Because people do not take care of their properties. Take this analogy to the physical body. Some people are slums, and some people are well-to-do physically and mentally. Why? Because they take care of themselves.

I am not saying all patients who seek psychiatric help are demon-possessed. Neither am I saying that the therapist who gets involved in transference and counter-transference becomes demon-possessed. The point I am stressing is that transference does occur as documented, and transference of spirits does take place. I am not saying that by counseling people you will become demon-possessed. I am not saying that by helping people you are going to be like they are. I am saying that if you do not know the spiritual implications, you will end up in the ditch with them.

That does not mean that he who knows the Word of God and knows how it operates will be demon-possessed. He cannot be. I repeat, he cannot be. You can be demon-possessed only if you want to be. If you do not want to be, you will not be. You do not have to be afraid that those demons will jump on you.

God Does Not Control His People

The answer to the need of humanity is for Christian psychologists who are born again and Spirit-filled, who understand the spirit world and are able to teach their patients the difference between the soul, the spirit and the flesh, to give counsel to those who are mentally disturbed. The Bible says the love of God never fails. If we have a cure-all medicine that never fails, why don't we use more of it? If I discovered a medicine that would cure every cancer, would people be calling me? Certainly they would. Every person would be calling me for just a little bit of it. If a little dab will do you, then why don't we advertise God's medicine—the love that never fails?

No matter how mean a dog may be, if you keep throwing a bone to him, before long he will wag his tail when he sees you approaching; he knows you are not there to hurt him but to feed him.

If a psychologist or psychiatrist or counselor is Spirit-filled and understands the presence and workings of evil spirits, he will soon discern the presence of demons and exercise his authority by the Word. God has given us power to tread on serpents and scorpions and cast them out, and nothing shall harm us (see Luke 10:19). When you go into counseling, you have the Word to protect you. It does not matter what spirits the person has because you have power over them to cast them out. But deliverance does not mean that no further counseling is necessary. Deliverance is not a cure-all. Deliverance is an initial stage of setting a person free.

Counseling on the psychological and spiritual level is a very serious matter. It must be continued until a person knows within himself that he is free. Discrediting the importance of either is to do a disservice to human needs. If a person says, "Well, I got delivered. I don't need any more counseling. I don't need any more teaching," it is a deception. We constantly need the help of Jesus in our lives.

Good counseling necessitates certain requirements. I have certain policies that a counselee must abide by. I try to be very frank and lay it out for them to make the decision whether or not they will abide by these policies. If they refuse to, I cannot help them. As a counselor you must always grant your counselee the privilege of making a choice. You cannot make a choice for him. God does not make a choice for you. You have no right to make a choice for those whom you counsel. They must make the choice on their own, and they must abide by the policies you have set up.

When I am counseling, I require that all counselees be born again. They must be Spirit-filled. They must go to church. They must tithe. If they oppose any of these areas, I give them the best information I can. If they are not willing, I know it is not going to work. Right there is unwillingness to comply with your requests. If you are doing it for your own selfish gain, that is wrong. Your intent and purpose should be to help the counselee.

What if they do not comply and continually come back because they go to your church? What if they are rebellious so far as taking the Word and acting on it? Then you are wasting your time. Tell them so. I say to them, "You are wasting my time and I am wasting yours. When you decide you want to follow my instructions, then I am confident I can help you, but I am not going to let you waste my time." You have to set certain guidelines. That is why people sometimes do not understand. In three sessions you should be able to tell exactly what is happening. If you cannot tell in three sessions, something is wrong. You should be able to see progress. If there is no progress, something is not right. People seeking help have to be transparent. They have to be open. If they continue to come after three sessions, it is no longer counseling but therapy.

I say to them, "OK, I am going to tell you what you need to do. You tell me whether or not you are willing to do it so we have an understanding. I will determine your problem and tell you what the solution is." That is counseling. That is communicating. Therapy is different. With therapy you deal in specifics and continue teaching the person over a period of time. The person has to be taught as in school. You are trying to uproot all bad things and replace them with positive attitudes. At first you tell them what the problem is and how you are going to deal with it. Then you go ahead and do it. That is therapy.

In dealing with people you must not allow yourself to be hindered or pushed in a corner by what they say against you—the way you operate, the way you counsel or the way you charge. Your purpose is to help them. When you recognize what they are saying and who is saying it, then you will be able to deal with it. God will use you to be a blessing. That is why it is important to realize the man at Gadara did not go to the Pharisees or the Sadducees. He came to Jesus. The individuals who call and say, "I don't want this God business" are not crying out for help. Learn to understand where they are coming from, and try to get them in for counseling. When you get them in, God can work with them.

Mark 5:7 says, "And [he] cried with a loud voice, and said, What have I do to with thee, Jesus, thou Son of the most high God? I adjure thee by God, that thou torment me not." Jesus could torment the devil and his demons. You can torment the devil and demons with the Word of God. "For he said unto him, Come out of the man, thou unclean spirit. And he asked him, What is thy name? And he answered, saying, My name is Legion: for we are many" (vv. 8-9). You can see by this that demons are knowledgeable— able to talk, answer and ask questions. "And he besought him much that he would not send them away out of the country" (v. 10). Did you know that you can send them out of the city? We can command demons to leave the city. "Now there was there nigh unto the mountains a great herd of swine feeding. And all the devils besought him, saying, Send us into the swine, that we may enter into them. And forthwith Jesus gave them leave. And the unclean spirits went out, and entered into the swine: and the herd ran violently down a steep place into the sea, (they were about two thousand;) and were choked in the sea" (vv. 11-13). This illustrates what the devil's final goal is. It is to destroy you. "And they that fed the swine fled, and told it in the city, and in the country. And they went out to see what it was that was done. And they come to Jesus, and see him that was possessed with the devil, and had the legion, sitting, and clothed, and in his right mind: and they were afraid" (vv. 14-15). The man who was possessed and not able to be tamed sat fully clothed and in his right mind when Jesus got through with him.

God's answer to the Gadarene man's problem is available to all who will cry out to Him and call on His name. It does not matter what the problem may be; the power of God is greater than the power of the devil. Even though the power of the devil can bind a man and cause him to hurt himself, when God gets through with that man, he is free.

The Bible says when those who came from the city saw the man in his right mind, they were afraid. Those demons also knew that something could happen to them. They were shaking in their boots. The demons were afraid, not the people. They did not ask for help. The demons knew that if they (the people) asked Jesus for help, He would cast them (the demons) out as well. The people did not ask, and He did not cast the spirits out. So you see that Jesus did not go around casting demons out of every person—only those who asked, and they were all around Him.

You do not force yourself on anyone, but you help those who ask. There is a danger in that. You do not want to give the devil an opportunity to make fun of you or think that you are not good enough to help them. When God is with you and someone asks for help, then you will see the miracles of God.

CHAPTER FIVE

Walk After the Spirit

In our study of transference and counter-transference of spirits, we have mentioned that if a counselor or therapist does not understand the spiritual implication of why people do certain things, there is no way he can help. The following news item which appeared in one of the local newspapers will back up my statement.

RAPE SUSPECT SHOOTS HIMSELF AFTER CHASE

A rape suspect who accidentally shot himself after a car chase ending in a crash was in serious condition at the local hospital Thursday afternoon, a hospital official said. A sheriff's spokesman said the suspect shot himself as he was about to fire at a deputy who had cornered him on Wednesday. Authorities were looking for a man in connection with a sexual battery report on Tuesday, said a spokesman for the County Sheriff's Department.

It was reported that a suspect was holding a teenager captive for five hours and sexually assaulting her. The victim's stepfather, who was at the shooting scene, said that the suspect is the girl's uncle. He said the family took him in after he was released from prison following a sex crime conviction. The man said that the suspect raped the girl at an orange grove Tuesday, then tried to rape her again at their home while holding her at knife-point. When the girl's brother walked in, the suspect grabbed his shotgun and left, the man said.

The suspect was charged with sexual battery and aggravated assault. The Sheriff's Department said other weapons charges would also be filed.

Here is a situation where a man who was accused and convicted of rape and sent to prison was determined to be rehabilitated after counseling and therapy. He behaved himself, so he was released. When he was released, he saw a woman, attacked her, raped her and was going to rape her again.

Is this man free? No! We can see that this man just came out of prison and was taken in by people who wanted to help him out. What happens? He again becomes a prisoner of the spirit that is on the inside of him. It is obvious he does not want to get caught. He is now worse than a rapist. He is a dangerous man with a weapon, thinking of taking others' lives.

Finding Freedom from Oppression

As I shared with you in the last several chapters regarding people who are demon-oppressed, you can suppress the spirit.

People can play the part. They can be so nice and smooth. No matter how much medication you give them, no matter how long you may keep them in prison, no matter how long you have them locked up, when they are released and the circumstances are right, those spirits will manifest themselves if the people have not been delivered. Now the rapist will not only rape but attempt to kill anyone who stands in his way. He is worse now than he was in the beginning because he knows he does not want to go back to prison.

If the man who rapes again does not want to go back to prison, why does he commit the crime? The flesh may desire to have a sexual release, but it is obvious he doesn't want a jail term. The only solution would be to have genuine biblical deliverance by casting out the spirits.

Just because you are a born-again Christian does not mean all of your problems are solved. As a matter of fact, they will start to intensify and come to the surface. You will have to know how to deal with these problems and demonic activities. I am not attributing everything to demons. However, if there is a habit in one's life, and the person is not able to control that habit, it is obvious that a demon is at work. A lot of this is fleshly. You can say no to the flesh, but much of the time the flesh gives in. With the man in the article, the flesh was unable to be controlled. You can see that this man was demon-controlled; the flesh gave in, and he did things he would not normally do if he had been delivered. Let's examine 1 Corinthians 2 and focus on several areas of the spirit of which you need to be aware. We are going to discuss transference of good spirits first, and then we will discuss transference of bad spirits and who transfers these spirits. Human beings are involved in the transference of spirits.

We who are Christians and have Jesus in us do not have to be afraid that these demons or spirits will jump on us. When we are washed with the blood and are walking in the right attitude, not lusting or desiring these bad spirits, they cannot transfer to us. We have to invite them. We can be assured we are safe under the blood of Jesus Christ and in His light if we walk in His light.

The problem much of the time is that people, even Christians, do not have knowledge in these areas. Because of the lack of knowledge we walk into situations and do not know how to get out of them. We are going to attempt to show you how you get into these situations and how to go through them without being tormented by evil spirits.

Choosing the Truth

First Corinthians 2:9 says, "But as it is written, Eye hath not seen, nor ear heard, neither have entered into the heart of man, the things which God hath prepared for them that love him." Most of us cannot comprehend what God has for us. The world, especially, cannot comprehend because it does not know what God has in store. Let me explain to you why the world does not understand. Indeed, even many Christians do not have the knowledge of what God has for them.

First Timothy 4:1 says, "Now the Spirit speaketh expressly, that in the latter times..." If people depart from the Word, it does not matter who they are. They may be Christians. Let's turn to John 3. I am going to show you why if they depart from faith they depart from the Word. If they depart from the Word, they depart from the truth. If they depart from the truth, they cannot teach the truth.

Let's start in John 3:17 and see why many Christians do not accept what the Bible says and why they give excuses for why it is not for today. The Word makes a demand on you. The Word will either get you to accept and follow Jesus and comply with His teachings or else you will deny the Word and the truth of it. People say, "Well, it is not for today. It is not for everybody. It was for believers in the past." The Bible is very clear. Keep these passages in mind: 1 Corinthians 2:9 and 1 Timothy 4:1.

Let's go to John 3:17. "For God sent not his Son into the world to condemn the world; but that the world through him might be saved." God's purpose is that the world be saved through Him. He is not teaching about the earth. He is teaching about the people in the world. Verse 18 says, "He that believeth on him..." Who's Him? Jesus, or the Word. In order to believe you have to have faith. "He that believeth on him is not condemned: but he that believeth not is condemned already, because he hath not believed in the name of the only begotten Son of God." Verse 19 says, "And this is the condemnation, that light is come into the world, and men loved darkness..." This is Jesus speaking. He is speaking to believers. "... And men loved darkness rather than light, because their deeds were evil."

He says in verse 20, "For every one that doeth evil hateth the light..." Who is the light? Jesus. Who is Jesus? He is the Word. Who is the Word? The Word is the Son of God. He says, "For every one that doeth evil..." That includes you and me and everybody else. If you do evil and not what the Word says, you are going to justify why you should not do what the Word says. You will find an excuse. If you do not have the knowledge of God's healing power that is available to every believer, you are going to say, "It is not for today," because you know that when you pray nothing happens. The reason nothing happens is you do not have the faith for it to happen. You must have faith. If your faith has departed, you are going to justify why it is not happening today for everyone. "Oh, it's for some, but not for everyone," you will say. I say to you that the Word is for everyone. Jesus says, "...that the world might be saved." He did not say just some of the world. He said the whole world may be saved.

People will also say, "Well, yes, we believe that Paul is preaching about the baptism of the Holy Spirit with the evidence of speaking in tongues, but it is not for us today." They deny the truth simply because they do not have the experience. You cannot teach something that you yourself do not know about. When you do not have the light on a subject, you are not able to bring forth the light to others. If men are honest, they will admit their lack of knowledge and say, "Yes, it's there, but I don't understand it. I need for someone to teach me." They do not want to say that because it will make them look bad in the eyes of men, and they do not want to lower themselves, especially if they are denominational pastors. They do not want to say they do not know something because they could lose their job and their retirement as well. To some it is a job, not a ministry. When you, as a child of God, do not know something, say, "Praise God, I have the Holy Spirit, and, brother, if you know something I don't know, please teach me. I want to know more. If it is in the Bible, I want to understand it. I want what God has for me." The Bible says the Word of God is "to admonish, to teach, to reprove, and to correct." When we as Christians accept that, we will be able to flow in the Word.

John 3:20 says, "For everyone that doeth evil hateth the light, neither cometh to the light..." Why? "...Lest his deeds should be reproved." That's strong. "But he that doeth truth cometh to the light, that his deeds may be made manifest, that they are wrought in God" (v. 21). Those who want the truth will come to the light and acknowledge the fact that all of this is a result of God's power and grace at work in them.

First Timothy 4:1: "Now the Spirit speaketh expressly, that in the latter times some shall depart from the faith, giving heed to seducing spirits, and doctrines of devils."

Second Peter 2:1: "But there were false prophets also among the people, even as there shall be false teachers among you, who privily shall bring in damnable heresies, even denying the Lord that bought them, and bring upon themselves swift destruction." Today we have people who say, "Well, the virgin birth of Christ is just a story; it didn't really happen that way. Christ was just another man." They do not even deny that He was a prophet, a good teacher. When you start pinning them down as to whether or not He is the Son of God, they say, "Well, I wouldn't go that far. I wouldn't say that." Well, I am saying that. Jesus is God. Jesus is the Son of God. Because He is the Son of God, these false prophets will deny Him as Lord.

"And many shall follow their pernicious ways..." (2 Pet. 2:2). You say, "How could they?" Because false prophets speak some truth, but they are still false prophets. As I said to you before, if you speak 99.9 percent truth but 0.1 percent lie, the whole thing is a lie. God's Word is not 99.9 percent truth. God's Word is 100 percent truth, and there is no lie in it. There is no darkness in it. My friend, either you are going to go all the way with the Word or you are not. If you deny one chapter in the Bible, you have denied the whole book. "If you deny any part of Me, you deny all of Me, not just part of Me," said Jesus. If you deny any part of the Holy Spirit and attribute any of the Word of the Holy Spirit to the devil, you have denied the Holy Spirit completely, and that is sin that the Bible says is not pardonable.

"And many shall follow their pernicious ways; by reason of whom the way of truth shall be evil spoken of. And through covetousness shall they with feigned words make merchandise of you: whose judgment now of a long time lingereth not, and their damnation slumbereth not. For if God spared not the angels that sinned, but cast them down to hell, and delivered them into chains of darkness, to be reserved unto judgment; and spared not the old world, but saved Noah the eighth person, a preacher of righteousness, bringing in the flood upon the world of the ungodly..." (2 Pet. 2:2-5).

If God did not spare the angels that sinned, He is not going to spare the false prophets or anyone who is entangled with them. The Bible is very clear. God is not going to put up with nonsense. We are either going to teach the Word and become His prophets or we will teach lies and become false prophets. The Bible says in Matthew 25:41 that hell was not prepared for people but for the devil and his angels.

Let's look again at 1 Timothy 4:1-2. "Now the Spirit speaketh expressly, that in the latter times some shall depart from the faith, giving heed to seducing spirits, and doctrines of devils; speaking lies in hypocrisy; having their conscience seared with a hot iron."

Ephesians 4:18-24 says, "...Having the understanding darkened, being alienated from the life of God through the ignorance that is in them, because of the blindness of their heart: Who being past feeling have given themselves over unto lasciviousness, to work all uncleanness with greediness. But ye have not so learned Christ; if so be that ye have heard him, and have been taught by him, as the truth is in Jesus: That ye put off concerning the former conversation the old man, which is corrupt according to the deceitful lusts; and be renewed in the spirit of your mind; and that ye put on the new man, which after God is created in righteousness and true holiness."

As believers we have a choice. We have a choice to either put on Christ and walk after the Spirit in true holiness or walk after false prophets and be deceived (covetous and lustful as the world is covetous and lustful). There are three spirits: the spirit of man, the Spirit of God and the spirit of the world.

First Corinthians 2:10-12 says, "But God hath revealed them unto us by his Spirit...." We see that God is a Spirit. "...By his Spirit; for the Spirit searcheth all things, yea, the deep things of God. For what man knoweth the things of a man, save the spirit of man which is in him?" The spirit of man is in the man. "...Even so the things of God knoweth no man, but the Spirit of God." So we have the spirit of man and the Spirit of God. The Bible says, "Now faith is...." "Now we have received...." Don't read forward into the word "not," because it is separated by a comma. "Now we have received...." What have we received? Skip the commas, and it reads, "Now we have received...the spirit which is of God." We have excluded what is set off by commas.

It is clear we have received something. In order for you to receive, someone has to give it to you. What have we received? We can receive the Spirit of God or the spirit of the world. The Bible says, "Now we have received...the spirit which is of God; that we might know the things that are freely given to us of God."

Receiving the Spirit

When we receive the Spirit of God we open ourselves up to receive what God has for us. When we come to God and ask Him, His Spirit will then be transferred into our spirit. Our spirit is capable of receiving not just the Spirit of God but also the mind of God, the heart of God, the Word of God, the message of God and the revelations of God. Our spirit is able to receive by means of the Holy Spirit and illuminate our intellect, whereby our intellect and our spirit are now able to receive His teachings. We say, "Why didn't I think of that?" Because our mind was not illuminated until we asked the Holy Spirit to show us. The Holy Spirit takes the mind of God, the wisdom of God, the mysteries of God and the Word of God and plants it in our spirit. Our human spirit and God's Spirit are working together, giving us the understanding and illumination. That is why Jesus was able to say, "My Father and I, We are one. What My Father does, I do likewise." Can you see why He was able to say that? Jesus and the Father were one. Because He had God's Spirit, Jesus was able to receive from God and not from the world. That is why He makes an emphasis here. "Now we have received, not the spirit of the world, but the spirit which is of God."

When you ask God's Spirit and His revelation to come into your life, it is not from the world. However, He did not exclude that. You can receive the spirit of the world as well. But when you ask God, your spirit will be filled by the Spirit of God. Your spirit and God's Spirit are then able to communicate, because God pours His Spirit into your spirit, so to speak. You then become spirit-filled. When you are spirit-filled, your spirit is able to receive God's transmission.

To make it more real in our everyday lives, let me use a radio transmission as an example. AM radio does not transmit FM waves. AM radio transmits AM waves or signals. An FM radio does not receive AM transmissions. AM radio stations send out AM radio waves that require an AM receiver. The AM receiver has to be turned on in order for you to receive what the AM station is sending. If you want to receive an FM signal, you must be tuned in to an FM radio station that transmits FM signals. In order for you to have a picture on your television screen, you have to tune in to that particular channel. You may have a television in your room. It may be hooked up. But if you do not turn to the right channel, you will not receive that channel's transmission.

You are in essence a receiver. God is the sender. He sends messages, and you are able to receive those messages. I don't know how it works, but it works. Can you imagine sending signals through the air and all of a sudden you turn the channel and the picture comes on? Isn't that beautiful? When God sends His transmission to you, listen. Do not miss it. When God sends His message into your tube, your receiver is capable of making pictures inside. Then everybody who tunes in and watches can enjoy the picture. What kind of picture do you show?

The Spirit of God is able to transmit. I do not understand how a television works because I have not studied it and all its intricate facets, but I know it works. I accept it. I do not have to fight it. I enjoy it. I may not understand how it works, but I do not have to know to believe it. It's right there. Turn it on. Likewise, when the power of God operates in you, don't say, "I don't believe that." Enjoy it. It's right there. It is available. Don't say, "I don't believe healing is for everybody." It is there. Turn it on and enjoy it. Why fight it? Some folks are still using the black and white picture. They say, "Well, that's the first thing that came out, and we're going to hold on to it." They could be receiving in full color.

Paul is saying in verse 12, "...We have received, not the spirit of the world, but the spirit which is of God; that we might know the things that are freely given to us of God." We see, then, that for us to receive from God, our spirit has to be in tune.

"Which things also we speak, not in the words which man's wisdom teacheth, but which the Holy Ghost teacheth; comparing spiritual things with spiritual" (1 Cor. 2:13). You cannot compare carnal things with spiritual things or vice versa. You must compare spiritual things with spiritual things.

"But the natural man receiveth not the things of the Spirit of God: for they are foolishness unto him: neither can he know them, because they are spiritually discerned" (v. 14). A man can be born again, but if he does not understand that he has to tune his spiritual receiver to the right channel, to him it will be foolishness. It is foolishness because to him the truth has not been revealed, and he will walk in darkness. Yet, to a degree, he loves God because his spirit is born again. That part has been revealed to him, and he has received it. However, the rest of it has not come to him because he is not willing to open himself up. You have to be willing to open yourself up for the Holy Spirit to reveal the mysteries of God in your life.

Verse 14 says, "...They [the mysteries of God] are foolishness unto [the natural man]." He did not say you have to be a heathen. He did not say this is foolishness to the heathen. It is to the natural man. Man can be born again and rely only on his intellect and knowledge. That is a natural man. However, the Bible says, "Lean not on your own understanding, but trust in the Lord." If a man does not know to lean on God and receive from God, he will always lean on his own natural senses. The natural senses are good to a degree, but they are not spiritual. They are not able to discern spiritual things. You will say, "Yes, this is a table, and it's hard. I know that." But you cannot perceive that before this table came into existence, it was already in God's heart to make trees. God spoke from the Spirit first before everything came into the natural world. All things are in the spirit realm before they come into the natural world. The Bible says God took the clay and formed a body. He breathed into that clay, and it became a living soul. It is obvious there was life before He created the natural thing. It only became alive when God was through with it. The same is true with everything around us. The pulpit, the wood of which it is made, everything that went into it was in the heart of God in the spirit realm before it came into being in the natural. The only thing we have to do is speak it into existence. As we speak it forth it becomes natural rather than supernatural. But it is in the supernatural, the spirit realm, first.

"But he that is spiritual judgeth all things, yet he himself is judged of no man. For who hath known the mind of the Lord, that he may instruct him? But we have the mind of Christ" (vv. 15-16). It does not say we have the mind of Jesus. It says we have the mind of Christ.

There is a difference between having the mind of Jesus and having the mind of Christ. To have the mind of Jesus would be natural, human. To have the mind of Christ is supernatural.

We see then that those who are in the Spirit and walking in the Spirit have the mind of Christ. They have the ability to receive from God the mysteries of God and apply them to their natural lives here on this earth. You have to see everything as being in the spirit realm first.

Having said this, we now see that there are three separate spirits: the spirit of man, the Spirit of God and the spirit of the world. The Spirit of God and the spirit of man can be joined together. The spirit of the world and the spirit of man can be joined together. Spirits (both good and evil) can be transferred to the human spirit.

Walking Together for the Glory of God

Numbers 11 says that the great anointing that was upon Moses was placed upon the seventy elders, and they prophesied. The Spirit came from the Lord upon Moses. From Moses, the Lord took the spirit that was upon him and gave it to the seventy. If they were to be of one mind, of one accord, of one spirit, they had to have the same spirit. The men who would work with Moses had to have the spirit of Moses, the vision of Moses and the desire of Moses in order to flow with him. Where this does not happen you will find discord, division, separation, accusation, argument, jealousy, bitterness, strife and false reports. For example, in a church or fellowship a pastor, assistant pastor, associate pastor, music pastor or youth pastor can come in and have a contrary spirit. We just witnessed this not long ago in a fairly large denominational church that went through a split. That does not bring glory to God. God can take the tragedy out of it and salvage much of it. But in the meantime the devil has a heyday and laughs at Christians. In essence he mocks God. We have to be very wise and not allow that spirit to manifest in us. It is better to have three faithful disciples than three thousand unfaithful disciples.

Numbers 11:16: "And the Lord said unto Moses, Gather unto me seventy men of the elders of Israel, whom thou knowest to be the elders of the people, and officers over them; and bring them unto the tabernacle of the congregation, that they may stand there with thee." I want you to see this. This is beautiful. "...Whom thou knowest..." You pick them out, Moses. I am not going to do the picking. You pick them out. You have been with them. You know them. You have seen their behavior. You go and pick these elders from among the people, men that you think are capable of handling responsibilities. Identify yourself with them, and let them identify themselves with you.

"And I will come down and talk with thee there: and I will take of the spirit which is upon thee, and will put it upon them" (v. 17). God says He will take it (the spirit) off and He will put it on. That is a transference of spirits. God is taking the spirit He gave to Moses—that spirit of power, authority, responsibility, vision, burden, concern and love—and putting it upon them. He is taking from one and placing it on the others.

You cannot deplete God's power. The elders' spirit would be like Moses' spirit, so whatever God put on Moses' heart would also be impressed upon the elders. God says, "I am going to cause strength, unity and oneness to come into your midst, because you are going to be of one spirit."

God knew everything, but He wanted a man to be involved in selecting those people with whom he would work. You may find a person who knows the Word, but you may not be able to work with him. Why allow someone to come in if you can't work with him? You have to have people who will submit themselves to authority and flow together to accomplish one goal—to bring glory to God. Some people are contrary. You give them a little responsibility, and they get cocky; they think they can run the whole show. They want to take the captain's chair. Make sure the people you select are well-seasoned so they will bring glory to God.

I do not know how old these seventy elders were, but they apparently had been leaders in their own tribal groups.

"And I will come down and talk with thee there: and I will take of the spirit which is upon thee, and will put it upon them; and they shall bear the burden of the people with thee, that thou bear it not thyself alone" (v. 17). Isn't that beautiful? God says, "I am going to cause them to flow together. You are going to be as one." Those of you who understand mechanics know how this operates. An engine may have eight cylinders, six cylinders or four cylinders, but every cylinder in that engine works for one purpose—to produce power. Every cylinder goes up and down in the engine. The shaft to which those cylinders are attached is there for one thing, and that is to move the vehicle or equipment. The cylinders work together in harmony. If one fails, the whole thing fails. That shaft may be one, but it has to be strong to crank the whole mechanism in order to move the vehicle. The cylinders produce the power in order for the whole automobile to move forward.

In essence, God was saying, "Moses, you are going to be the shaft. You are going to keep these elders in line. But they are going to take the burden in moving this whole congregation. They will be the ones whom I will distribute power upon, and yet you will control the entire power."

Let me show you another example of the transference of good spirits, this time under the new covenant. Turn to Acts 6. Let's compare and see how similar this is. It is important that we flow in the same vein and compare spiritual things with spiritual as the Bible teaches us.

Acts 6:1 says, "And in those days, when the number of the disciples was multiplied, there arose a murmuring of the Grecians against the Hebrews, because their widows were neglected in the daily ministration." There arose a murmuring. There was disharmony of spirit. The people were murmuring among themselves. They were dissatisfied. Whenever you have dissatisfaction, you are going to have bickering and upset people.

"Then the twelve called the multitude of the disciples unto them, and said, It is not reason that we should leave the word of God, and serve tables" (v. 2). It is obvious to me that there are two categories here. There were separate responsibilities—serving tables and ministering to the people, and also trying to receive from God direction for the people. The disciples said, "We have our assignment. We have our responsibility."

"Wherefore, brethren, look ye out among you seven men"—or choose you out seven men—"of honest report, full of the Holy Ghost and wisdom, whom we may appoint over this business." He says, "We are going to let you go among your own selves and choose." That is scriptural, right? You go among yourselves and choose seven men "...of honest report, full of the Holy Ghost and wisdom, whom we may appoint over this business. But we will give ourselves continually to prayer, and to the ministry of the word. And the saying pleased the whole multitude: and they chose Stephen, a man full of faith and of the Holy Ghost, and Philip..." (vv. 3-5). These men had proved themselves to be honest, full of wisdom, full of the Holy Ghost and power. What I want you to understand is that they did not choose men who just had the power. They chose men who were honest. They chose men who had good reputations in the community as well as the power of the Holy Spirit.

Jesus said, "But ye shall receive power, after that the Holy Ghost is come upon you" (Acts 1:8). It is important for us to choose men, not because they are well-to-do or influential, but because they are honest. More than that, they love God with all their heart, and they are full of the Holy Ghost and power. You can be influential and honest, but if you have no power, what good is your influence? God is not impressed with how much influence you have in the community. God is impressed with how full your heart is of His Spirit. If your heart is full of His Spirit, He will give you favor with men in the community. It is a beautiful thing to know that God gives you favor.

Let's look at Acts 6:6-7. "...Whom they set before the apostles: and when they had prayed, they laid their hands on them. And the word of God increased;..." I am convinced that when the burdens are lifted from the pastor and others are able to take them, God's Word will increase in the congregation. If the pastor is burdened down with all the responsibilities of the congregation, the Word of God decreases. These apostles were bold enough to say, "That's not our job. That's not our responsibility. We are to be in the Word, and we are to fellowship with the Lord and increase the Word in the body. We will select men whom we trust, full of the Holy Ghost, who are able to receive from God. They can do these things while we get the Word out. When we get the Word to you and the Word increases, everybody is going to be blessed." If you stop the Word from increasing, everyone is deprived of the blessings of the Lord.

Verses 7 and 8: "And the word of God increased; and the number of the disciples multiplied in Jerusalem greatly; and a great company of the priests were obedient to the faith. And Stephen, full of faith and power, did great wonders and miracles among the people." I like that. Stephen, who was chosen by God, did great miracles and wonders among the people. Wouldn't it be wonderful for a pastor to take a person in the congregation and put him in a position of responsibility he could be trusted with? When that happens, think how many more people we can touch. Think how many lives can be blessed when there is no suspicious spirit, no fear, no backbiting or criticism. If we will magnify the Lord Jesus and have the same spirit no matter where we are, there will be no room for bickering. We will not allow a spirit of division to come in and separate us. That is being led, and that is being filled by a good spirit. When we have that kind of transference in our lives, we will affect people in a way the world has never experienced. Only those who are in the Spirit and walk in the light know the peace that passes all understanding. This is what happens when we walk in the same spirit.

We need to be alert. We need to be on guard. We need to be full of the Holy Spirit and power. We should not allow another power to manifest in our midst, or even within our hearing. Just put that fire out. Do you know that 90 percent of my time is spent putting out little fires? Think what it would be like if I spent 90 percent of my time ministering to the Lord and being in the Word. Think how much more I could do if I was able to devote 100 percent.

I am convinced there are many pastors who are doing their best to preach to a congregation, but most of their time is spent putting out little fires. A little bickering here, a little bickering there, a little division here, a little criticism there, a little lie here, a little adultery there. They try to put out all these little fires in an attempt to keep the body together. Think what would happen if all of us had the same spirit. Think what would happen if we had seventy elders in our church (or even seven), full of the Holy Ghost and power, who would be the eyes and ears for Jesus, ministering the Word. Wonders and miracles would follow.

Many times a young congregation has to import people who have been trained by someone else. They come from different backgrounds, different denominations. They haven't been raised up in the same body. Such a person may bring outside ideas, and sometimes that's good. But much of the time it is not good. When you import outside help, you also import outside problems. If that person who comes in is not flowing in the same spirit, be it a minister, a music minister, a Sunday school teacher or a children's church minister, rest assured that spirit is going to cause problems. That spirit has to be removed. When you have "another spirit," it is very dangerous.

The phrase "another spirit" is used in Numbers 14. We find it in the story of the twelve spies sent by Moses to spy out the land: "Surely they shall not see the land which I sware unto their fathers, neither shall any of them that provoked me see it: But my servant Caleb, because he had another spirit with him, and hath followed me fully, him will I bring into the land whereinto he went; and his seed shall possess it" (vv. 23-24).

When a person has another spirit and is not able to flow with the vision God has given you, that spirit causes problems. Very few are able to divest themselves of this other spirit, and most do not even know they are under the guidance of another spirit.

Some will say, "Is there such a thing?" Yes, there is such a thing. I have just shown you Scripture stating there is such a thing.

There is another spirit, even among those who are in the same congregation. Caleb and Joshua and the ten came back with two different spirits. God is telling us that these spirits are real.

Now turn to Isaiah 61:1-3. "The spirit of the Lord God is upon me; because the Lord hath anointed me to preach good tidings unto the meek; he hath sent me to bind up the brokenhearted, to proclaim liberty to the captives, and the opening of the prison to them that are bound; to proclaim the acceptable year of the Lord, and the day of vengeance of our God; to comfort all that mourn; to appoint unto them that mourn in Zion, to give unto them beauty for ashes, the oil of joy for mourning, the garment of praise for the spirit of heaviness; that they might be called trees of righteousness, the planting of the Lord, that he might be glorified." The spirit of joy is there to glorify the Lord.

The prophet Isaiah said, "The spirit of the Lord God is upon me; because the Lord hath anointed me..." Did you know that the ministry of Jesus did not begin until the anointing came? Did you know that our ministry will not begin until the anointing comes? The anointing is upon the Word, and when Jesus was full of the Word He went out into the wilderness and was tempted by the devil. The Bible says the Word came out of Him. He said, "Man shall not live by bread alone, but by every word that proceedeth out of the mouth of God." Jesus was full of God's Word, and whatever temptation came His way, the only thing that came out of His mouth was the Word which caused the devil to back off.

The same thing is going to happen to you and to me when we receive the Spirit of God into our lives and are full of God's Word. When we open our mouths, we will not say, "Well, look at those circumstances. How are we going to pay those bills?" The anointing will break the yoke. God is going to supply, God is going to multiply, God is going to cause the circumstances to diminish. His power increases as we stand upon His Word.

I encourage you, as you minister, to discern what spirits are in operation. Only when we are aware of these things are we able to identify them. Test the spirits. Walk confidently and boldly, and know who you are in Christ. When you walk with the Lord Jesus, you have His Spirit upon your life, and nothing shall harm you.

HEREDITARY TRAITS

CHAPTER SIX

Be Not Deceived

There are certain things that the Lord will do that we cannot do, and there are certain things that we can do that the Lord will not do. Recently while I was praying, the Lord dropped something in my spirit. I knew it all the time, but it came alive. I was asking the Lord, "Why is it that so often Christians know the Word and can quote the Word, and yet the devil comes in and steals, kills and destroys?" Here is what the Spirit of God said. "If the devil cannot deceive you, he cannot rob you. He cannot rob you of your finances or your family or your happiness." God showed me that when the devil deceived Eve, he robbed her of her relationship with God. If the devil cannot deceive you, he cannot rob you. That means you have to have revelation knowledge so that when temptation comes you will know how to shut the devil out.

The Bible says, "I give you power to tread on serpents and scorpions." If the devil can deceive you and say, "Who do you think you are? How are you going to bless people when you do not have any money? How are you going to invite people over when you cannot even buy food for yourself?" he will deprive you. Close the door on him. I want you to keep that in your spirit and help someone else with it. We all need to be aware that if the devil cannot deceive us, he cannot deprive us.

Recently revelation knowledge came to me. It happened so fast it seemed unreal. I had been praying for a friend who was financially strapped. The Lord told me that where there is an ounce of fear, the person will not receive the blessing. He told me to tell the person to go ahead and write the checks out, address the envelopes, put stamps on them and expect a miracle.

The same thing is true of tithing. Many people tithe 10 percent of what they receive. That is scriptural; however, many people only tithe what they have. There is no faith involved. When a person tithes 10 percent he is giving back to God what God has already given him. It belongs to God, not the tither. What we should do is tithe on what we expect to receive. That is where faith comes in. That is when God really blesses. It is like a farmer sowing one acre of corn. He is going to get a one-acre harvest. But if he says, "I am going to plant two acres," he will receive a larger harvest. Until now he has only planted one area. Now he says, "I am going to expand. I am going to believe that I can plant two acres." He plants two acres. He does not know how he is going to do it, but he believes for it. God gives the seed to the sower.

There Is Only One Head and One Body

We are dealing with transference of a good spirit. Let's think about a good spirit for a moment. The person who is in tune with God and ministers to the people of God will always feed a relationship with another person. That other person will always receive from him because he trusts him. He will become like him and get his vision. He will get his spirit. Some of his gestures will be like the teacher's. Their expressions will be similar. On the other hand, if that person goes elsewhere into the ministry and takes the spirit with him, he may have a conflict in the new area with people who do not go along with his spirit. Realize that even though people love God they still have opinions, and their own will is involved. Let me show you an example.

I asked a Spirit-filled, ordained minister to reserve certain seats for a meeting. I did not go into detail about why I wanted this done. That person took it upon himself not to do what I had requested. When I got to the meeting, the places which I wanted reserved were not reserved. I asked the minister why he did not do what I had asked him to do. He said that in his opinion it was unscriptural. He said the Scriptures say we are not to be respecters of persons. I told him I did not care about his opinion; I wanted him to do what I had asked him to do.

Because he came from somewhere else and was taught differently, he brought with him a different opinion. When the situation presented itself, a wrong spirit manifested.

Before I fired him, I explained why I wanted the seats reserved. They were reserved for ministers and counselors whom I needed to minister to the multitudes. Jesus had twelve disciples by Him. He had a place reserved for them so He could use them to minister to the multitudes. We are not respecters of persons, but we need people to minister to others. I asked that these seats be reserved for that purpose.

I had to dismiss that spirit immediately. You may say, "Why didn't you give him another chance?" Chances had been given before in other things. I finally had to deal with the person and dismiss him. Why are there schisms among believers in the body of Christ? Why are there separations? Why do we find disagreement among believers?

The answer is simple. Because these people are not of the same spirit as the leader (see Amos 3:3). First Corinthians 6:17 says, "But he that is joined unto the Lord is one spirit." If we are one in the Lord, we must be one in the spirit. If we are in His Spirit, then we are also one in the Lord.

Moses had quite a few Israelites under his supervision. God took Moses' spirit and placed it on the seventy elders. When the spirit of Moses was upon them, they were all of one spirit and one mind.

When people are in one spirit they are in submission one to another. They never fight the leader. If the leader is wrong, they pray for him. They care enough about him to not talk and backbite. They don't leave notes on the outside of his door. They always look for an opportunity to bless, uplift and help the leader. Their ultimate goal is to allow the leader to be a blessing to people and thereby glorify God.

When people are in one spirit they accept and understand authority. A Roman centurion said, "I understand authority because I am a man of authority. Because I am a man of authority, I say unto this man 'Do,' and he does. I say unto this man 'Go,' and he goes." (See Matt. 8:1-13.) Therefore he said, "Jesus, You speak the word, You be my commander, and I will do exactly what You say, because I understand authority. I am willing to submit myself to authority." That is being in one spirit. A centurion who was not even a Jew understood the principle of authority and unity and the strength it provides. He did not question Jesus. He did not oppose Him or criticize Him.

Those who are in one spirit work for the benefit of the whole. They are not selfish or jealous. They are not envious. Those who are flowing in one spirit have a priority that is not self but rather the whole body of Christ. They are concerned about how something will affect and minister to the whole body of Christ.

Those who have the same spirit as the leader never start their own groups. They support their leader even as the seventy elders supported Moses all the days of his life.

As you examine churches and religious organizations of today, you will soon see that authority is either in operation or it is lacking. When it is in operation, strong churches numbering into the thousands often result. The church staff admire and respect the senior pastor almost to the point of imitating him. When you find people in a congregation who are in one spirit, you will see that congregation prosper, and you will see the Shekinah glory of God emanating through and from them. As leaders we must be of one spirit, one vision and one determination. That is for the good of the whole, to further the body of Christ.

When you have a strong-willed associate or administrator come on staff with another vision, another spirit, soon there will be followers who will ultimately be divided in their loyalties and destinies. This is not only in churches. This occurs in businesses, marriages and families.

Rebellion Against Godly Principles Is Sin

Today many of the churches in the body of Christ teach about government by plurality and leadership of co-equal eldership. I have never discovered in the Bible that democracy is sanctioned by God. God never had two leaders of equal rank leading a group of people. God always had one leader.

Every time the children of Israel decided on a democracy, whether it was fostered by Miriam, Aaron, Korah, Dathan or Abiram, it always brought God's judgment.

The Bible speaks of the church in Laodicea, which was ruled by the people. It was condemned by the Lord because God's government is not democracy; it is theocracy. Let's look at Numbers 16:1-11 and 17-21. "Now Korah, the son of Izhar, the son of Kohath, the son of Levi, and Dathan and Abiram, the sons of Eliab, and On, the son of Peleth, sons of Reuben, took men: And they rose up before Moses, with certain of the children of Israel, two hundred and fifty princes of the assembly, famous in the congregation, men of renown" (vv. 1-2).

These are very important verses. These men had been chosen. They were admired and looked up to.

91

"And they gathered themselves together against Moses and against Aaron, and said unto them, Ye take too much upon you, seeing all the congregation are holy, every one of them, and the Lord is among them: wherefore then lift ye up yourselves above the congregation of the Lord? And when Moses heard it, he fell upon his face: And he spake unto Korah and unto all his company, saying, Even to morrow the Lord will shew who are his, and who is holy; and will cause him to come near unto him: even him whom he hath chosen will he cause to come near unto him. This do; Take you censers, Korah, and all his company; and put fire therein, and put incense in them before the Lord to morrow: and it shall be that the man whom the Lord doth choose, he shall be holy: ye take too much upon you, ye sons of Levi" (vv. 3-7).

The sons of Levi were chosen to minister. They had a ministry ordained by God; however, a wrong spirit was at work in them. It is important to see from this story how a wrong spirit can destroy a person and get him away from a good spirit by allowing jealousy and envy to come in. These were renowned men. They had position. They were called by God. They had already been appointed to minister to God's people. But they were not satisfied. They began to develop their own group. There were 250 already gathered.

"And Moses said unto Korah, Hear, I pray you, ye sons of Levi: Seemeth it but a small thing unto you, that the God of Israel hath separated you from the congregation of Israel, to bring you near to himself to do the service of the tabernacle of the Lord, and to stand before the congregation to minister unto them? And he hath brought thee near to him, and all thy brethren the sons of Levi with thee: and seek ye the priesthood also?" (vv. 8-10).

These men were not satisfied with what God had called them to do. They wanted someone else's calling. You cannot go after someone else's calling or someone else's spirit. That spirit must be given to you by God. These men were trying to seek the position of Moses—a position that God did not call them to. He called them to a specific job. When God calls you to a position, be satisfied. If

God has called you to be a counselor, be a counselor. If He has called you to be a wife, be a wife. If He has called you to be a pastor, be a pastor. If He has called you to be an evangelist, be an evangelist. Whatever God calls you to do, be satisfied in that position. Do not try to take over. "For which cause both thou and all thy company are gathered together against the Lord: and what is Aaron, that ye murmur against him?" (v.11).

Moses was saying, "Why are you murmuring against Aaron? Who is he? Why should you do that?" Versus 17-21 say, "And take every man his censer, and put incense in them, and bring ye before the Lord every man his censer, two hundred and fifty censers; thou also, and Aaron, each of you his censer. And they took every man his censer, and put fire in them, and laid incense thereon, and stood in the door of the tabernacle of the congregation with Moses and Aaron. And Korah gathered all the congregation against them unto the door of the tabernacle of the congregation: and the glory of the Lord appeared unto all the congregation. And the Lord spake unto Moses and Aaron, saying, Separate yourselves from among this congregation, that I may consume them in a moment."

I want you to grasp how powerful this is. So often people ask how they will know the truth if we do not minister to them. These people knew the truth, but a wrong spirit got into them. God brought judgment upon the people with the bad spirit, but He gave aid to those who were with Moses.

The Bible teaches that you cannot fight against God and win. It would be foolish to try. But the devil is just that stupid. He will do anything. He will still try to take the power away from God's anointed.

God said, "Get away from these people with the wrong spirit because I am going to consume them." If you do not get away, what will happen to you? You will also be consumed because you did not obey.

Wrong Spirit Brings Destruction

Learn a lesson here. When you have discovered a wrong spirit, do not get involved. Do not try to be God. Do not try to save them. Turn them over to God. Get away from the situation, and God will spare and protect you. He says to separate from them while they are consumed. You might ask, "Will God consume today?" God is still God. He still hates sin and rebellion. Those people may not die immediately, but spiritually they are already dead. Verse 22 says, "And they fell upon their faces, and said, O God, the God of the spirits of all flesh, shall one man sin, and wilt thou be wroth with all the congregation?"

Do you see the boldness of Moses in speaking to God like that? Wouldn't it be well if you and I learned to be bold as well? God is your Father. He is your Friend. God called Abraham His friend. I believe you ought to be honest before your Friend. I believe you ought to be able to speak before your Friend. If you cannot speak to your Friend, who can you talk to? Moses said to God, "You can't do that!" It's about time we learned how men of old spoke to God. They were not being rude but knew that God is God. They were friends of God, His servants, and they had a right to talk to Him. They were not afraid. They knew what God would do and what He would not do.

"And the Lord spake unto Moses, saying, Speak unto the congregation, saying, Get you up from about the tabernacle of Korah, Dathan, and Abiram. And Moses rose up and went unto Dathan and Abiram; and the elders of Israel followed him. And he spake unto the congregation, saying, Depart, I pray you, from the tents of these wicked men, and touch nothing of theirs, lest ye be consumed in all their sins" (vv. 23-26).

Rebellion is sin. When a person rebels, whether it is in marriage, business or the church, there is a wrong spirit. Disagreement and separation result. Korah had been delivered out of bondage just like Moses and the other elders. But he said, "Who do you think you are, Moses?" No man can elevate himself unless God puts him there. Only God promotes (Psalm 75:6-7). These men had taken it upon themselves to do that. God says He will destroy them if they continue to associate with evil men.

"So they gat up from the tabernacle of Korah, Dathan, and Abiram, on every side: and Dathan and Abiram came out, and stood in the door of their tents, and their wives, and their sons, and their little children. And Moses said, Hereby ye shall know that the Lord hath sent me to do all these works; for I have not done them of mine own mind. If these men die the common death of all men, or if they be visited after the visitation of all men; then the Lord hath not sent me. But if the Lord make a new thing, and the earth open her mouth, and the earth swallow them up, with all that appertain unto them, and they go down quick into the pit; then ye shall understand that these men have provoked the Lord.

"And it came to pass, as he had made an end of speaking all these words, that the ground clave asunder that was under them: And the earth opened her mouth, and swallowed them up, and their houses, and all the men that appertained unto Korah, and all their goods. They, and all that appertained to them, went down alive into the pit, and the earth closed upon them: and they perished from among the congregation. And all Israel that were round about them fled at the cry of them: for they said, Lest the earth swallow us up also. And there came out a fire from the Lord, and consumed the two hundred and fifty men that offered incense. And the Lord spake unto Moses, saying, Speak unto Eleazar the son of Aaron the priest, that he take up the censers out of the burning, and scatter thou the fire yonder; for they are hallowed. The censers of these sinners against their own souls, let them make broad plates for a covering of the altar: for they offered them before the Lord, therefore they are hallowed: and they shall be a sign unto the children of Israel" (vv. 27-38).

Now that is a very powerful message. We see how a person with a good spirit becomes a person with a wrong spirit. When the congregation takes it upon itself to make decisions, statements, comments, judgments and criticisms without God's direction, it is sin. Be careful that you do not allow this to happen in your congregation. It will spread like a cancer, and it will anger God. When God says He will remove the chaff from the wheat, He will do it. But He will keep the wheat because that is the seed that will produce the harvest.

"But on the morrow all the congregation of the children of Israel murmured against Moses and against Aaron, saying, Ye have killed the people of the Lord. And it came to pass, when the congregation was gathered against Moses and against Aaron, that they looked toward the tabernacle of the congregation: and, behold, the cloud covered it, and the glory of the Lord appeared. And Moses and Aaron came before the tabernacle of the congregation. And the Lord spake unto Moses, saying, Get you up from among this congregation, that I may consume them as in a moment. And they fell upon their faces" (vv. 41-45).

God was coming down to consume the entire Hebrew congregation except Moses and Aaron and their families. He was not going to put up with that spirit. He would allow it to go no further. He was willing to make a nation of people who would obey Him from Moses and Aaron. When God cleans His house, He cleans it well.

When God saw these people complain against Moses, He released the spirit of plague. He gave that spirit an opportunity to go and consume them. We know that God does not destroy. The devil is the destroyer. God is the life-giver. When God lifts His hand off a congregation, the devil comes in like a thief and wipes it out. God lifted His hand from this congregation. Aaron stood before God and the congregation and offered an atonement for the people.

I want you to see how quickly the devil operates. If you allow someone to murmur in the congregation, it will go through the congregation like a plague and destroy innocent people. It will consume them and wipe them out. You who are counselors and leaders must always be on guard and stand between evil and the congregation so the plague will not consume them. The spirit of evil is a plague. It will destroy a marriage, a business or any other relationship. If you allow people to continue with a negative attitude, it will cause a good spirit to suffer. Good people can be consumed because of ignorance, not knowing what the spirit is doing through them. The Bible says Moses recognized the plague as sin and sent Aaron to intercede. Aaron stood between the living and the dead and God, and the plague was stayed.

"Now they that died in the plague were fourteen thousand and seven hundred, beside them that died about the matter of Korah. And Aaron returned unto Moses unto the door of the tabernacle of the congregation: and the plague was stayed" (vv. 49-50).

Those who leave congregations without the pastor's blessing and God's blessing, who leave angry and start their own fellowship, will entreat others to join them. They have a wrong spirit. What kind of spirit did they leave? What kind of spirit is in them? There is a danger. You could be involved just as those innocent people who were wiped out by the plague simply because they were in a congregation of complainers. They may not have complained themselves, but because they were in the congregation of complainers, God said He was going to wipe them all out. Praise God for Moses and Aaron and their compassion for the people. They stood between the destruction and God because they were pure. They were chosen by God and anointed by God. Because of one man standing between God and an evil congregation and asking God to forgive them, the rest of the congregation was spared.

Jesus is our high priest. First Timothy 2:5 says, "For there is one God, and one mediator between God and men, the man Christ Jesus." Notice he did not say Joseph Smith. He did not say Buddha. He did not say Mohammed. He said "...the man Christ Jesus." Buddha did not defeat the devil. Neither did Mohammed or Joseph Smith. When Jesus fought the devil, He did not fight him as deity. He fought him as a man. That is why He can relate to you and me. That is why He is our intercessor. That is why He is our mediator. That is why He is able to stand between God and man and keep death and the plague from destroying us even by the sins of other people. The blood of Jesus Christ will not allow sin to cross the boundaries. God set the boundary. Where the blood is applied, sin cannot pass through. Whenever you do wrong, forsake that activity and repent; you are immediately covered by the blood. Jesus Christ, the Righteous One, stands before God, and God will not lift His hand against you. Instead He will lift His hand to redeem you and set you free from plague and destruction.

The New Testament churches gave birth to Paul's apostolic ministry. We see him constantly at the helm of every church that was started under his ministry. He was not a roaming minister; he was the one who started the churches. He had authority over all those churches while elders were in submission to his apostolic ministry. If they had a doctrinal matter to settle, they went to Paul.

The spirit that was upon Moses was upon the seventy. If they were going to assist Moses, they were going to need the spirit that was upon him. They were not taking over from him. They did not want his position. They were assisting and giving pastoral assistance to the people in the spirit of Moses. Those who are elders, deacons, board members and counselors in churches should allow in themselves only the spirit with which God has anointed their pastor. With the same pastoral care they become ministers.

Paul ministered only to those who were in charge. They were the ones who went out and ministered to the people. They had the responsibility. Paul taught them and brought the Word to them and made the decisions by which they abided.

If a church leader has the Spirit of God dwelling in him and a pastor, associate pastor or church officer recognizes and receives this spirit, you will witness strength, unity, joy and harmony operating in their midst. The enemy cannot penetrate such a spiritual force. The people will not allow a false spirit to rise up among them. They will put it down immediately. It is the same in the army. When a soldier detects a sniper in the area, his object is to remove the sniper. The sniper could kill anybody. So he alerts everyone to the danger, and everyone concentrates on removing the sniper so no damage will be done.

When the elders, deacons, pastors and staff work together with the congregation, they will bring peace, unity, cooperation, faithfulness and commitment among the people. They have to take it upon themselves to do that. A Sunday school superintendent or children's church pastor should impart into his teachers peace, unity, loyalty, honesty and cooperation so they will transmit these to the children. The children will receive that spirit in their classes. When the head teacher is not willing to abide by the rules, that teacher will eventually drop a hint here and there of a wrong attitude. Before long the children will pick it up and start talking like the teacher. Before you know it, the whole congregation will be like that teacher because the children go home and tell their parents. The parents will come in with the same spirit.

A wrong spirit brings destruction, but a good spirit brings peace and harmony.

When a particular chain of loyalty is broken, another spirit enters in and the breakdown takes place. Loyalty is strong only until a link has a contrary spirit. The great danger is that the contrary spirit can affect the connecting links unless that spirit is recognized and dealt with. I have seen it happen time and again in churches. A contrary spirit wreaks havoc in the kingdom of God. I have never seen a church, organization or marriage get broken from without. It is always broken from within. We need to be alert.

This also happens many times in ministries. When a pastor or ministry has a wrong spirit and you sit under that teaching, it is possible for you to have the wrong spirit. It is dangerous for young Christians to jump from meeting to meeting, from pastor to pastor, from church to church. The reason we have so many people church-hopping is because of the spirits involved. When a person is grounded in the Lord, he is not going to move from place to place. Many of the people who go from church to church and meeting to meeting are very unstable. You can understand why. They are tormented. They do not have peace. They get a little from this one, a little from that one, and before long they have a spiritual smorgasbord. It can be a mess. We need to be careful about our intake.

CHAPTER SEVEN

Be Ye of Good Courage

The children of Israel came out of Egypt, seeing many miracles along the way. God had promised to take them to a land flowing with milk and honey, where all their needs would be met. In Numbers 13-14 we find the Israelites camped in the wilderness of Paran. They devised a plan to send twelve spies to determine whether Canaan was indeed a good land. Already they were making a mistake. God had told them it was a good land that flowed with milk and honey. They did not always follow God through their trek in the wilderness.

Numbers 13:1-3 says, "And the Lord spake unto Moses, saying, Send thou men, that they may search the land of Canaan, which I give unto the children of Israel: of every tribe of their fathers shall ye send a man, every one a ruler among them. And Moses by the commandment of the Lord sent them from the wilderness of Paran: all those men were heads of the children of Israel."

Why were they sent? Because of their natural qualifications. They had honor in their families, in their tribes and in the whole house of Israel. They were prosperous. They were leaders.

The passage in Numbers 13:4-16 gives us the names and tribes of the twelve spies. One of these men was Joshua. Joshua is a term used throughout the Bible referring to Jesus as well. As a matter of fact, the Scriptures often refer to Jesus as Joshua, especially when speaking prophetically in the Old Testament.

The spies did not bring back a good report. We have learned that the enemy comes in and sows tares among the wheat, choking out the fruit. They are those who gossip and do detrimental things, causing themselves and others to backslide. In the list of spies, there is one name that stands out.

In verse 13 we find Sethur, the son of Michael, mentioned. This name comes directly from the Hebrew word *sathur*, which means "to conceal" or "to hide." It also has a numerical value of 666, which is the number of the Antichrist found in Revelation. We cannot say he was strictly responsible for the evil report brought back, but the meaning of his name is very interesting. We also know that people in the Old Testament seemed to follow their destiny according to their names.

The word used to name Abraham's father means "delay." Abraham left the city of Ur in the Chaldees when God called him out. But he was a little slow getting to the land of Canaan because his father was holding him back.

When we name our children we should take into consideration the meaning of the name. There is power in a name. When we are called by a name, many times we manifest the characteristics of that name. Just as we speak the Word and expect things to come to pass, when people speak our name, they are producing spiritual power. It is a word of spirit and life or a word of spirit and death. There are many undesirable names. Look closely at what names mean in the Old and New Testaments. Many times a person's name will point toward certain characteristics.

Someone among the spies had a wrong spirit. A negative spirit can start with just one person. Jesus said, "Beware of the leaven of the Pharisees" (Matt. 16:6). In 1 Corinthians 5:6 Paul warned that "a little leaven leaveneth the whole lump." It could have taken only one person to start the negative report that the spies brought back. Let's see what the Word has to say about it.

In verse 16 Moses renamed Oshea, calling him Johoshua, or Joshua: "And Moses sent them to spy out the land of Canaan, and said unto them, Get you up this way southward, and go up into the mountain: And see the land, what it is; and the people that dwelleth therein, whether they be strong or weak, few or many; and what the land is that they dwell in, whether it be good or bad; and what cities they be that they dwell in, whether in tents, or in strong holds; and what the land is, whether it be fat or lean, whether there be wood therein, or not. And be ye of good courage, and bring of the fruit of the land" (vv. 17-20).

In Joshua 1:6 Moses gave the exhortation to Joshua and the other spies, "Be strong and of a good courage: for unto this people shalt thou divide for an inheritance the land, which I sware unto their fathers to give them." In verse 7 and again in verse 9 the same thing is stated.

What You Fail to Conquer Will Conquer You

Moses gave instructions in Numbers 13 to be strong, courageous and positive. As we approach any situation we must be strong and courageous and not allow the spirit of fear to enter in. Moses was aware that the spies might see some frightening things, so he gave specific commands to be strong and courageous before they went into the land of Canaan.

Numbers 13:20-22 goes on to say, "... And be ye of good courage, and bring of the fruit of the land. Now the time was the time of the firstripe grapes. So they went up, and searched the land from the wilderness of Zin unto Rehob, as men come to Hamath. And they ascended by the south, and came unto Hebron; where Ahiman, Sheshai, and Talmai, the children of Anak, were. (Now Hebron was built seven years before Zoan in Egypt.)"

Hebron was a place where Abraham also dwelt. If you are familiar with your Old Testament history you know that Abraham lived there. In fact, he and his whole family were buried in the caves of Machpelah near Hebron. Since the children of Israel had left the land, the sons of Anak had taken over Hebron.

The sons of Anak were extraordinarily large and powerful people, what we would call giants. It is interesting that Hebron, a place once visited by God, had been taken over by enemies of God. The very place where Abraham lived and dwelt and was later buried had become a dwelling place of people committed to evil. No longer was the name of the Lord used there.

"And they came unto the brook of Eshcol, and cut down from thence a branch with one cluster of grapes, and they bare it between two upon a staff; and they brought of the pomegranates, and of the figs" (v. 23).

Those clusters of grapes weighed between twenty-five and forty-five pounds and were called plums because they were so large. Israel is most definitely a land flowing with milk and honey! The blessings of God are upon it. When the Israelites saw the huge grape cluster, it was proof that the land was full of blessing.

"The place was called the brook Eshcol, because of the cluster of grapes which the children of Israel cut down from thence. And they returned from searching of the land after forty days" (vv. 24-25).

In forty days the advance party had plenty of time to search the land from one end to the other and make their determination. But at some point someone began to listen to the enemy. As we read on we find that a certain spirit had already taken hold of them. It says in verses 26-27, "And they went and came to Moses, and to Aaron, and to all the congregation of the children of Israel, unto the wilderness of Paran, to Kadesh; and brought back word unto them, and unto all the congregation, and shewed them the fruit of the land. And they told him, and said, We came unto the land whither thou sentest us, and surely it floweth with milk and honey; and this is the fruit of it."

Verse 28 says *nevertheless.* This word is our signal that something negative and contrary to what God had said is about to follow: "Nevertheless the people be strong that dwell in the land, and the cities are walled, and very great: and moreover we saw the children of Anak there."

Note one of the devil's characteristics. He did not hinder the spies from returning, nor did he hinder them from bringing back fruit from the land. As a matter of fact, he made sure those spies made it back to give the evil report. He saw to it that they brought back the fruit just so he could tempt the people and then tell them they could not take the land. This is a typical tactic of the enemy, one that we need to be aware of. Bring in a sample of the fruit, show it to the people and tell them this is all they are going to have—this is what the devil will do in our individual lives unless we confront him through spiritual warfare. When a spirit of despair and defeat comes, will will never enjoy the fullest blessings God has for us unless we are strong in our faith.

The children of Israel had the potential to receive every blessing of the land that God had for them. However, they did not receive because they listened to the evil report and the negative spirit that was transferred to them.

"The Amalekites dwell in the land of the south: and the Hittites, and the Jebusites, and the Amorites, dwell in the mountains: and the Canaanites dwell by the sea, and by the coast of Jordan" (v. 29).

Here is a consistent evil report. There is one pack of devils here and another pack of devils over there. These reports made sure everybody knew just how impossible the situation appeared to the eye. "Yes, the land is good, but we cannot have it. We will not enjoy it." That is the same line the devil sells people today. It affects individuals, ministries and churches alike.

"And Caleb stilled the people before Moses..." (v. 30). I am sure Caleb said the equivalent of "shut up!" He realized that negative words would never bear good fruit. "And Caleb stilled the people before Moses, and said, Let us go up at once, and possess it; for we are well able to overcome it. But the men that went up with him said, We be not able to go up against the people; for they are stronger than we" (vv. 30-31).

The Bible says that out of the abundance of the heart the mouth speaks. Already their hearts and minds had been undermined by some double agent planted in their midst who said they were not able. During the forty days and nights the scouts were gone, the infection of the enemy plagued all but two with doubt. People are still under this influence today. People tend to lean toward the negative rather than the positive. They gravitate toward hearing those things which are evil rather than those things which are good. If a major minister of the gospel went to Africa and 240,000 people came to know the Lord, would it be reported in the news? No. However, if that minister were found guilty of adultery, you'd better believe it would be in the news. People look for the negative because of the spirit of the world.

Caleb told the Israelites they were able to overcome. But the popular report was that the giants were stronger. The negative people, the devil's bunch, had already determined there was no way they could do it. They agreed that the land was flowing with milk and honey, but *nevertheless* they wanted to tell the negative. That is often how a negative spirit enters in.

The movie *Mary Poppins* featured a song called "A Spoonful of Sugar Makes the Medicine Go Down." The devil uses the same tactic with believers. He will say, "Yes, you need all the benefits that God has for you, but if you get the baptism of the Holy Spirit and begin to speak in tongues, people will say you're weird. They will kick you out of your church. Your family will not like you anymore. Yes, there are blessings there, but think about what you are going to have to suffer if you try for them."

Very rarely does the enemy come out and say, "You can't do it." Instead he tries to divert our attention to the negative. After a while the spies dropped the pretense concerning the goodness of the land. You will usually see this pattern in people who bring an evil report. When they become filled with that negative spirit, they drop any pretense of the positive. We find in verse 32 that the spies' report has become totally negative—nothing positive, nothing good.

Earlier the spies had reported it was a land flowing with milk and honey. All of a sudden the land itself had become a terror that would destroy the people who tried to take it.

You Are What You Think

As a man thinketh in his heart, so is he. If we allow negative thoughts to permeate our minds, we become that thing we meditate upon, and everyone else will regard us as such. The people of the land looked at the children of Israel and said they were as grasshoppers. Why? Because the Israelites had determined within themselves this was the way it was to be. They took that bondage upon themselves. God did not lay it on them. He did not say they were weak. Moses had charged them to be strong and of good courage. They saw themselves as grasshoppers.

One of my favorite questions when people are against the wall is, "Are you a giant-slayer or a grasshopper?" There are a lot of grasshoppers in the body of Christ today. They go to one church, come up against the wall, don't like it and hop to another church. They go from city to city and never accomplish anything because they never overcome their fear. A negative spirit has entered into them.

When an evil report is first given, the devil usually sweetens it to make it a little more palatable. Later on there is no pretense of anything sweet. Solomon said this about wine: "It looks nice and red in the cup, but if you drink too much of it, at the end it stings like an asp and it bites like an adder." The same is true with an evil report. If you receive it, even mixed with a bit of sweetness, eventually it will turn to bitterness. It will cause great difficulty.

Jesus said we are overcomers through the blood of the Lamb and the word of our testimony. That is our identity. We are not failures. Jesus did not die to produce failures. He died so that He could spread His winning Spirit among all of us. He has called us overcomers and said that nothing will be impossible to us. We must see ourselves as overcomers. Even though the children of Israel had the testimony of miracles, they allowed that negative report to enter in.

The children of Israel did not have the advantage we have in being born again and one in the Spirit with Christ. They did not have the Word of God readily accessible in the Bible. The Word of God was kept shut up. Everything was transmitted through the priests (Aaron and his sons) and Moses, who knew the Word of God. Miracles alone will not keep our relationship with God fresh. Having a relationship with Jesus Christ through His Word keeps us free. We can draw a parallel to the children of Israel in the wilderness. They received manna every day. They had daily provision from God. Even though they did not have the Word of God, they did have that daily testimony that God was caring for them.

Jesus is the Rock. Moses was not supposed to strike the rock. He was supposed to speak to the rock. Because he struck the rock in disobedience, he was not able to enter the promised land. Jesus was the Rock, the Bread of Life that came down from heaven. He was the water that came out of the rock. The Israelites had a daily testimony that God was there. At night a pillar of fire went before them, and during the day, a pillar of cloud. They had these constant reminders of God.

Romans 1 says that no man is without excuse because the invisible attributes of God have been around since the beginning. Creation itself proclaims the glory of God and witnesses to His power. What about unreached peoples in remote places? The Bible says if you seek the Lord you will find Him. The truth of God's Word is revealed in His creation.

Even with all these benefits, the children of Israel still brought forth the evil report concerning the land. They allowed the negative spirit of the world to be transferred to them, producing the evil report.

Numbers 14:1 says, "And all the congregation lifted up their voice, and cried; and the people wept that night." They could have been rejoicing. They could have been celebrating, preparing to receive what God had given them. Instead they wept because they allowed themselves to be poisoned with the evil report. As a result, the spirit of the world was transferred to them.

"And all the children of Israel murmured against Moses and against Aaron: and the whole congregation said unto them, Would God that we had died in the land of Egypt! or would God we had died in this wilderness!" (v. 2).

Then came the spirit of suicide. The people were despairing. They had listened to the evil report. It permeated their minds. Then they began to speak about death. When the spirit of death comes in, it causes people to contemplate destroying their own lives.

Let's look a little bit further and see what happened. Verse 3 says, "And wherefore hath the Lord brought us unto this land, to fall by the sword, that our wives and our children should be a prey? were it not better for us to return into Egypt?" Had any wives and children disappeared? No. Had any armies come up against them? No.

Hindsight is always 20/20. The past suddenly looks better when we are faced with the uncertainty of the future. With God there is no uncertainty. There is a surety that He will deliver us. "For as many that call upon the name of the Lord will be saved."

"And they said one to another, Let us make a captain, and let us return into Egypt" (v. 4).

Now that makes a lot of sense, doesn't it? They had just wiped out the entire Egyptian army, which didn't exactly earn them Brownie points. God had delivered their firstborn children from the death angel in Egypt, and now they wanted to return to the Egyptian people, who hated them.

"Then Moses and Aaron fell on their faces before all the assembly of the congregation of the children of Israel" (v. 5). Moses and Aaron, being leaders, knew what had to be done. They fell on their faces and began to pray.

"And Joshua the son of Nun, and Caleb the son of Jephunneh, which were of them that searched the land, rent their clothes" (v. 6). Here were the only two men among all the spies who had a righteous attitude. "And they spake unto all the company of the children of Israel, saying, The land, which we passed through to search it, is an exceeding good land" (v. 7).

Verse 8 says, "If the Lord delight in us, then he will bring us into this land, and give it us; a land which floweth with milk and honey." Here again we have the resurgence of the good report, brought by the two men who were righteous. They were not involved in the murmuring. They were not involved in the death talk. They were ready to bring a good report. In verse 9 they point out the situation: "Only rebel not ye against the Lord, neither fear ye the people of the land; for they are bread for us: their defence is departed from them, and the Lord is with us: fear them not."

"But all the congregation bade stone them with stones" (v. 10). Here is the spirit of death again. Now they want to murder. First they wish they were dead. Then they contemplate killing and murdering those who speak the truth. Verse 10 continues, "And the glory of the Lord appeared in the tabernacle of the congregation before all the children of Israel."

"And the Lord said unto Moses, How long will this people provoke me? and how long will it be ere they believe me, for all the signs which I have shewed among them? I will smite them with the pestilence, and disinherit them, and will make of thee a greater nation and mightier than they" (vv. 11-12).

Let me point out that what God was offering to Moses and Aaron was a very exciting proposition. God was saying, "I will just get rid of these people and make a nation out of you." That would have been very tempting if Moses and Aaron had only been seeking to exalt themselves. But look at what happened.

"And Moses said unto the Lord, Then the Egyptians shall hear it, (for thou broughtest up this people in thy might from among them;) And they will tell it to the inhabitants of this land: for they have heard that thou Lord art among this people, that thou Lord art seen face to face, and that thy cloud standeth over them, and that thou goest before them, by day time in a pillar of a cloud, and in a pillar of fire by night. Now if thou shalt kill all this people as one man, then the nations which have heard the fame of thee will speak, saying, Because the Lord was not able to bring this people into the land which he sware unto them, therefore he hath slain them in the wilderness. And now, I beseech thee, let the power of my Lord be great, according as thou hast spoken, saying, The Lord is longsuffering, and of great mercy, forgiving iniquity and transgression, and by no means clearing the guilty, visiting the iniquity of the fathers upon the children unto the third and fourth generation. Pardon, I beseech thee, the iniquity of this people according unto the greatness of thy mercy, and as thou hast forgiven this people, from Egypt even until now" (vv. 13-19).

Moses was standing between the people and God, interceding on their behalf. He did not accept the offer God had made. He did some straight talking with God. This man was not born again, but he was so convinced of his right and his covenant with God that he could speak to Him this way. When you are sure of your covenant rights and your standing with God, you can have this kind of conversation with God—not demanding that God do something for you, but standing on your covenant rights. Moses was simply reminding God of His promise and His own character. This is something we need to do as well. The Bible says, "Put him in remembrance; let us plead together that you may be justified." We can come boldly before the throne of grace. Moses was not afraid to make this statement. Look at the results in verse 20:

"And the Lord said, I have pardoned according to thy word: But as truly as I live, all the earth shall be filled with the glory of the Lord. Because all those men which have seen my glory, and my miracles, which I did in Egypt and in the wilderness, and have tempted me now these ten times, and have not hearkened to my voice: Surely they shall not see the land which I sware unto their fathers, neither shall any of them that provoked me see it: But my servant Caleb, because he had another spirit with him, and hath followed me fully, him will I bring into the land whereinto he went; and his seed shall possess it" (vv. 20-24).

Caleb did not have the spirit of the world; rather, he kept the spirit of God. He was of another spirit. Of course, Joshua was of the same spirit as Caleb, and brought forth a good report. God said every person who had rebelled against Him would not enter into the land of Canaan. The Israelites wandered in the wilderness for forty years before they entered into the land of Canaan. During those forty years each person of that generation who rebelled against God died. It was a new generation that passed over into the land, with the exception of Caleb and Joshua, who had brought forth a good report.

There are some lessons to be gleaned from this. Many times people are at variance with their leaders. Then the vision is not accomplished. God loves these people, but He moves them all out and brings others in so that the vision may be completed. I have seen God turn over entire congregations and bring in entirely new congregations to help the leaders accomplish His vision. God will bring in people to go into the promised land.

A conspiracy always starts with one individual who listens to the enemy and then brings others into his camp. The same thing happened to the kingdom of David. When David was king, his son Absalom rebelled and drew people away with him. He formed his own group to do his own thing.

The same thing happens in the kingdom of God today. People don't like what's going on, so they rebel against authority and often draw away, seeking their own group. They have their own home prayer meetings that become their own church, or they leave one church and start their own. Division in the body of Christ is not from God. God was not the initiator of denominations. He desires that the kingdom of God increase and the body of Christ grow. Because of dissension, denominations have come into being. It is not God's will to have many denominations, but He is using them to bring forth His Word. I believe God is bringing us all together in the unity of the faith described in Ephesians 4.

If you were a Levite, your employment was in the service of God. If you were a Levite of the sons of Aaron, you could be qualified for the priesthood and even the high priesthood. There is a difference between Levites who served as doorkeepers, those who carried the ark of the covenant and those who were responsible for handling the sacrifices. Everybody had his own job. We discussed this in a previous chapter. Korah rebelled against the leadership, God's anointed.

To stretch forth your hand against God's anointed is to do serious damage to yourself and others. God raises up leaders, and He will put them down if necessary. To take matters into your own hands is extremely dangerous, whether or not the individual in leadership is right or wrong. If leaders are wrong, we need to pray for them. We might even go and tell them our viewpoint, but it is not our place to assassinate their character or raise up others in rebellion against them. That is a transfer of the negative spirit of the world—the same spirit that came into Balaam and caused his ministry to end in ruin. The Bible says Satan "goes about as a roaring lion, seeking whom he may devour." Just as God searches the hearts of men looking for those who will be obedient to Him, even so the devil is at work finding those who will submit to his will. When we see rebellious groups forming and hear negative things being spoken against those in authority, we need to steer clear of those people and not be involved.

The word of God is a dividing line. There will always be those people who receive God's Word, act in accordance, hold it as holy and separate themselves, not holding to doctrines of men. Doctrines of men will profit nothing. They are temporal. The Word of God abides forever.

Many people in the ministry today have allowed the negative spirit of the world to come upon them; pride and hurt follow. Because of that they come in and seek a part that is not theirs. This doesn't mean God might not promote them to some other office, but in seeking an office that is not theirs they throw their ministry away. If you cannot succeed for God in the midst of the circumstances you have, you will not succeed anywhere else. A change of scenery will not help you succeed. The same spirit will come time and time again.

If someone in this situation opens himself up before God and repents, God will restore him. God says in His Word, "I will cause you to forget the shame of your youth." God does not want us to be bound by our past. He wants us to be free to live and to enjoy the future. He can even cause us to forget the shameful experiences of the past.

Under the old covenant individuals were not to touch those things that were declared unclean, lest they become ceremonially defiled. Because of the sin of Korah and his group, Moses instructed the people to come out from the midst of them and not touch any possession of theirs.

God brings restoration and forgiveness to those who repent and change. Elisha said to Elijah, "Let a double portion of your spirit be upon me." We know that a transference of spirits can happen in the positive realm as well as the negative. When you are a part of a group or congregation, the spirit of the leader will affect you as well. Be sure the leader follows after God and not his own selfish desires, because you are submitting to his leadership. If you do not feel your leader has the right spirit, find somewhere else to go.

HEREDITARY TRAITS

CHAPTER EIGHT

Be Filled with the Word

There are three parts of man: spirit, soul and body. These three individual parts make up the whole man. We are teaching about the psuche man. *Psuche* is a Greek word used as a root word for many of our English words, most notably psychology. Note the relationship. The *psuche* man is the natural (soul) man. When *psuche* is used in the New Testament, it generally means "natural life." God is referring to natural life or the things of the soul (the mind, will and emotions).

Several words are used for life in the New Testament, but the predominant words are *psuche* and *zoe*. Kenneth Hagin deals with this in his book *Zoe: The God Kind of Life. Zoe* means the God kind of life or eternal life. Whenever you see the phrases *eternal life, everlasting life* or *life of God* in the New Testament, they are being translated from the Greek word *zoe*. The word *life* is found many times in the Gospel of John. In it you will find a tremendous use of both *psuche* and *zoe*. This is because John was very interested in both the life of God and the natural life and how they are related to each other.

First of all we must understand how we receive and contact this natural realm. If we are going to receive from God, we must receive from Him in the spirit.

We do not receive from God through the soul; He communicates with us in the spirit realm. Our communication with God is Spirit to spirit. Our soul is then edified by the revelation knowledge we receive in our spirit. Have you ever been listening to something that suddenly came alive to you? That was revelation knowledge coming to life. It was not coming to life in your mind but was being birthed in your spirit. Many times the revelation knowledge we get from God seems illogical to the mind. Suppose you are in a financial bind and you receive revelation knowledge concerning tithing. You have all these bills due, but all of a sudden the inside of you says, "That's right. Tithing really makes sense." It doesn't make sense to the mind because the mind is saying, "What about the rent? What about the water bill? What about my responsibilities?" But you received revelation knowledge in your spirit. It was a direct communication from God to your spirit.

When we communicate with God in the spirit, that knowledge flows from our spirit into our soul. Then it affects the mind, and all three work together in harmony.

First Corinthians 2:11 says, "For what man knoweth the things of a man, save the spirit of man which is in him? even so the things of God knoweth no man, but the Spirit of God."

When a movie is projected, the film is put in the projector, the projector throws light through the film, and the picture appears on the screen where you can see and comprehend it. The projector, film and light must have a surface on which to project the image. When you receive revelation knowledge in your spirit, your spirit acts like the projector, which plays that knowledge into the area of your mind where you are able to understand it. The same process happens many times when we see visions inwardly. Such a vision is not seen with your physical eyes; rather, the vision or picture comes through your soul and into your mind. It does not originate in your mind. It comes from your spirit, but it is manifested in your mind. Your mind is the screen that receives revelation knowledge from God.

"Now we have received, not the spirit of the world, but the spirit which is of God; that we might know the things that are freely given to us of God" (1 Cor. 2:12).

God communicates with us the things that are of His Spirit. What things are of His Spirit? The Word of God. If you receive communication that is contrary to the Word of God, it is not a communication from God. God's communication with us is based upon His Word. God will never break His promise of fidelity by acting in a way that is contrary to His Word. He has declared that He is bound by His Word. He is the same today as He was yesterday. He is the same forever. He said, "Heaven and earth will pass away, but my word will never pass away."

When God imparts knowledge to our spirit, we are then able to recognize it with our mind. Our mind must be trained to receive revelation knowledge. That is why so many people have difficulty when they know that God speaks to them and gives them instruction. They still end up doing the same things they were doing before they got the instructions from God. This is because their minds have not been renewed. Let's take a look at what the Word has to say about renewing the mind.

First Corinthians 2:13 says, "Which things also we speak, not in the words which man's wisdom teacheth, but which the Holy Ghost teacheth; comparing spiritual things with spiritual." When we speak the Word of God and the revelation knowledge that God has given us, we speak not with the words we have gained from man's wisdom or the words we have gained from our intellect.

In the Greek language, the word *comparing* also means

"combining." God takes us, puts us together and combines the human spirit and the Spirit of God. It is a transference of spirits. The Holy Spirit transfers information to our spirit and we become one with Him.

Romans 8:16 says, "The Spirit itself beareth witness with our spirit, that we are the children of God."

In 1 Corinthians 2:13 we find that "...the Holy Ghost teacheth; comparing [combining] spiritual things with spiritual." The communication we have with God is based upon the relationship the Spirit of God has with our own human spirit.

"But the natural man receiveth not the things of the Spirit of God: for they are foolishness unto him: neither can he know them, because they are spiritually discerned" (v. 14). The natural man does not receive the things of God because they are perceived as ridiculous. They make no sense to him. If the natural man could receive the things of God, everyone would be saved. If the natural man could receive directly from the Spirit of God, everyone would see and understand the Word of God immediately. We know that in salvation the Holy Spirit must first draw those whom He is calling; then God gives them new birth in the Spirit, and they have communication with God. That communication with God begins with the Holy Spirit. That is why people try to form their own means of getting in touch with God. They meditate and suffocate in a mass of theology that has nothing to do with God's Word. Man's own approach to God springs from the soul.

The only way the natural man can flow with the things of the Spirit is by becoming renewed in God's Word. The Word says it is impossible for two to walk together unless they be agreed.

Second Corinthians 6:14-15 says, "Be ye not unequally yoked together with unbelievers: for what fellowship hath righteousness with unrighteousness? and what communion hath light with darkness? and what concord hath Christ with Belial?" Light and dark cannot fellowship; therefore, the spirit and soul are opposed to one another. Unless the soul is brought into submission, there will be constant tension between the two. If the soul and the spirit walk together hand in hand, great power can be released. If the soul and the spirit oppose one another, a lot of time is wasted and nothing is accomplished for the kingdom of God.

Continuing in 1 Corinthians 2:14, "...for they are foolishness unto him: neither can he know them, because they are spiritually discerned." The *psuche* man cannot receive or understand the things of God. All around us are people who have built their own denominations, their own cults and their own groups based upon their idea of how to understand God. Anyone who tries to interpret God through the mind will always come out with a perverted and distorted picture of Him and will not have a true relationship with Him. There is no way communication can be established except in the realm of the spirit.

God has made it possible for men's spirits to be renewed, recreated on the inside, so they can have fellowship with God. The old covenant was put into place to usher in the Messiah, Jesus of Nazareth, who through His death and final sacrifice shed His blood for our salvation and the renewal of our spirits.

People who are not born again have spirits that are under the domination of the world's system and therefore the enemy. Why is that? Because the enemy is active in the world. He is active in the realm of the soul. Jesus said to the scribes and the Pharisees, "You are of your father the devil." They said, "We are the children of Abraham." Jesus said, "No, you are of your father the devil, and his works you will do because he was a liar from the beginning."

John 10:11-18 gives a contrast between the words *psuche* and *zoe*: "I am the good shepherd: the good shepherd giveth his life for the sheep. But he that is an hireling, and not the shepherd, whose own the sheep are not, seeth the wolf coming, and leaveth the sheep, and fleeth: and the wolf catcheth them, and scattereth the sheep. The hireling fleeth, because he is an hireling, and careth not for the sheep. I am the good shepherd, and know my sheep, and am known of mine. As the Father knoweth me, even so know I the Father: and I lay down my life for the sheep. And other sheep I have, which are not of this fold: them also I must bring, and they shall hear my voice; and there shall be one fold, and one shepherd. Therefore doth my Father love me, because I lay down my life, that I might take it again. No man taketh it from me, but I lay it down of myself. I have power to lay it down, and I have power to take it again. This commandment have I received of my Father."

Jesus was saying that when we talk about the natural life it is about both the soul and the body. Let's deal with the soul realm. In order to be an effective minister, Jesus said, "If I am going to lead the sheep there are things I will have to do for the sake of the sheep. I am going to have to lay down my natural life and minister to them in the Spirit." Jesus also said this: "The foxes have their holes, the birds have their nests, but the Son of Man hath no place to lay his head." Jesus set aside certain natural benefits for the sake of being able to minister to the people. He set aside His natural life, the things of His soul. He put others' needs before His own. If we are going to minister to others effectively, we must be prepared to put their needs before our own.

Jesus often spent all night in prayer, and in the morning He went to where the people were. The first thing He did was heal the sick. There was hardly ever any rest. He did get away from time to time to pray, but the Bible says He constantly laid down His natural life, His right to do things He wanted, for the sake of those to whom He was ministering.

God wants you to prosper. He wants you to have the things you desire, but there are times when we must set aside things we enjoy for the sake of others. There are also times when we must set aside things we enjoy for the sake of our witness to others. Certain activities might be perfectly all right for us, but those same activities may have a harmful effect on others. By choice, then, we give up those activities.

What You Feed on Will Tell on You

In the New Testament a question Paul dealt with at length concerned whether or not it was all right to eat meat that had been offered to idols. At the time of the New Testament church there were no supermarkets. If you wanted to get meat, especially in a Greek city, the best place to find good meat was at the heathen temple. Sacrifices were held on a regular basis, and the priests sold meat on the side to profit the temple and to make sure everybody got their cut. After a sacrifice was offered, the meat was divided up and taken to the temple market, where it was sold. Among Christians there arose great contention about whether it was proper to eat meat that had been dedicated to an idol. Was it a fitting thing to do?

Meat dedicated to idols was looked upon by many Christians as unclean and not appropriate to eat, even if it was the best sirloin steak in town. If you happened to drive to the meat market at the Temple of Zeus, for example, and pick up a steak or two, people might start judging you, saying, "Why is he going into that heathen temple and buying that meat? Doesn't he know he is participating in a sacrifice to a heathen god?" We know that idols have no power in them. Wood has no power in it. Stone has no power in it. Just because it has been fashioned into the likeness of some bird or animal does not mean it has any power. Yet we do our best to avoid using those things that represent Satan and his cohorts. In other words, we do not want to see how close to the world we can live.

Buying meat was a big issue in the early church, and Paul said, "Look, we know that an idol is nothing and meat is nothing. All these things were created by God. The meat and the materials the idols are made of were created by God. Nevertheless, if my brother stumbles because of my eating meat, then I am not going to eat meat while the world stands."

If your freedom brings other people into bondage, is that really your freedom? Suppose your brother, who is weaker than you and

123

has a weaker conscience, sees you going to the temple meat market and leaving with your chuck roast. Because of that he figures it is all right to eat all the meat he wants and do anything he wants. He's free. He is not under bondage to the law anymore. He can do whatever he wishes, and he begins to live a life of sin because he has seen that you eat meat and thinks you can do anything you want.

We can relate this to any number of issues today. A big concern when I was in the Pentecostal church was whether you played cards or danced. Many other activities were also considered questionable. What we need to consider is that even though we may be free to do such things, are we giving a good witness for God? Are we setting a good example for others so that they do not look upon our freedom as an excuse to come into bondage?

There are things you might do in the company of your husband, your wife or your family that are perfectly all right, but they would not be a good thing for you to do in the midst of the congregation. You might be convinced those things are righteous, but for the sake of anyone who may come into confusion over it, you choose not to do those things in a crowd of people you do not know. You must always be thinking even as Jesus was thinking when He said, "I lay down my life for the sheep."

You Act on What Dominates Your Life

Some activities are definitely sinful and to be avoided. Other activities are not sinful in themselves, but if they are abused they can become sinful. Take drinking and eating, for example. Sipping a glass of wine is not sinful; getting drunk is. Eating food is not sinful; gluttony is. All these kinds of things do not start out to be bad in themselves, but if they are overdone and begin to control you, they can bring you as well as other people into bondage.

Jesus was willing to set aside the things of His natural life, even His right to sleep, for the sake of others. In doing that He was able to minister effectively.

When we set aside the things of the *psuche* man, we also become spirit-conscious. This means we sometimes do things that crucify the flesh in order to come into union with the Spirit of God. A good example is fasting. Doing without food for the purpose of spending time with God is good exercise for the spirit. It causes us to grow. The benefit of fasting very often does not come while you are fasting but when the fast is over. You have taken the time to dedicate a portion of your life to God and say, "Lord, I'm going to do without this." It doesn't have to be just food. It could be anything. It might be the newspaper. It might be TV. It might be anything you spend time with that you set aside for God. When you do that, the benefit comes after the fast. When you spend time edifying your spirit in communication with God, you become stronger spiritually.

Everyone should live a "fasted life" to begin with. Do not allow anything to control you. If there is something that controls you, fast until it loses its control over you. Once you have broken that control, which has been built up in the mind and sometimes by the interference of demonic forces, you are free to do as you will.

Kenneth Hagin once said he was never going to drink another Coke because when he was a young boy he used to drink "many, many Cokes a day." That's a lot of Cokes, isn't it? I found out I was drinking too many soft drinks. I realized it was possible for me to drink a six-pack a day. I was not doing it consciously. I just wanted something to drink, so I reached into the refrigerator at the office and just kept drinking all day. By the time a whole day had gone by, I had consumed who-knows-how-many ounces of Pepsi or Coke. Realizing this, I started to think, "You know, this really has control over me. I'm just drinking it unconsciously." I drink things other than soft drinks now. I occasionally have a soft drink, but I do not drink it like I used to because I refuse to let anything have a hold on my life. Coffee is another example. Everything God created is good, but if it controls you, it is not the spirit of God. Deal with it in that fashion. Jesus was always willing to lay down His life for the sake of others.

You Can Become What You Believe

John 12:25 says, "He that loveth his life [*psuche*, natural life, or soul; who worships his mind, or who worships his soul or the pleasures thereof] shall lose it; and he that hateth his life [*psuche*] in this world shall keep it unto life eternal [*zoe*]." This literally means that people who set aside the appetites of the mind, soul and flesh for the sake of the kingdom of God will gain eternal life. Not only will they gain eternal life in the future by going to heaven, but they will gain the blessings of eternal life now: health, prosperity and all the blessings of God.

If we do not allow the *psuche* to control us, we will inherit eternal life, the *zoe* life. Jesus said in Mark 10:29-30, "There is no man that hath left house, or brethren, or sisters, or father, or mother, or wife, or children, or lands, for my sake and the gospel's, but he shall receive an hundredfold now in this time, houses and brethren, and sisters, and mothers, and children, and lands, with persecutions; and in the world to come eternal life."

When you give up your natural *psuche* life for God, you gain zoe life from God. All the blessings and prosperity of a relationship with Him will then be poured out on you, and people will notice it. Everybody will know you are blessed. Some will get upset and persecute you. People may not like the fact that the pastor has a new house. They feel the pastor ought not to have a big house. A pastor ought not to have a Mercedes or a Lincoln.

People can look at you and know whether you are walking in God's Word. Either the fruit is there or it is not there. If the fruit is there, it is obvious to all that you are staying in God's Word. That does not mean you will not experience attacks from the enemy. No matter how prosperous you are, the devil will sometimes try to dry up your finances or attack your body.

There are many leaders in the religious community who have revelation knowledge and have been taught about the Holy Spirit. Yet they do not understand the things of the unholy spirit, Satan, and his demons. Another minister who professes boldly that he casts out demon spirits will often be criticized even by these respected leaders in the religious community.

When you come into a realization that there is a spiritual war raging all around us and that God has empowered us to cast out devils, be assured that many people will give you a rough time. Let the Spirit of God flow through you. If you step out in God's Word and do what is right, people will begin to take notice.

To the same extent that you step out in God's Word, you become a pioneer in your own life. Pioneering new territory always brings naysayers, those who say, "He's losing a grip," or "She doesn't have it all together." The same thing happens in the world when someone comes up with a new idea, a new invention or a new business: "It can't be done. It's impossible." That same spirit is at work in the church for those who catch hold of God's Word. When we discover that the Word of God is true and begin to deal with these spirits, someone will say, "It can't be done," or "That's not real." Jesus said, "All things are possible with God."

In ministering with regard to demon spirits and setting people free, you are always going to find individuals who contradict what you say because they do not accept it. That is just a fact of life, so you must be prepared to deal with it and not let it get you down.

Second Corinthians 4:18 says, "While we look not at the things which are seen, but at the things which are not seen: for the things which are seen are temporal; but the things which are not seen are eternal."

One day everything on earth will be burned. The whole world and all of its works, the Bible says, will be destroyed in a fervent heat. A new heaven and a new earth will take its place. The things of the spirit last forever, yet in the world the natural holds great sway over our lives. Those who do not have a relationship with God and do not understand the spirit realm can only look at life from their frame of reference, which is according to the *psuche* man. They do not understand that the things of the spirit are eternal and more powerful than the things of the world.

Hebrews 11 tells us that everything we see was created out of things we do not see. The spirit realm is always first. This is especially true in ministry. When you are dealing with a mentally oppressed person, look for the root of that oppression to see if a spirit is involved. If there is a sickness there, check to see if a spirit is causing the sickness. Everything we see in the natural was created from spiritual substance. It is law.

We must become conscious of the things that are eternal in order to walk in victory over the things of this world. A spiritual battle is going on all around us, and since the realm of the spirit is much more real than the realm of the natural, we must learn how to tap into its power. We contact that power in our own spirit working together with God's Spirit. The Spirit Himself beareth witness with our spirit that we are the children of God. We have that relationship with Him, and that gives us access to the power of God.

CHAPTER NINE

How To Control Your Thoughts

From time to time every believer has carnal thoughts and wrong attitudes. Once when I was about to minister, horrible carnal thoughts flooded my mind. I thought, "Dear Lord! Where did this come from? This is going to knock me out of the Spirit." That was the idea. The devil wanted to get my mind off God; he wanted to ruin that evening's ministry. Although my mind had been renewed in that area, still the thoughts came. The devil was seeking to bring about the destruction that comes from meditating on those particular things. To be tempted with a worldly thought is not sin; however, if you accept and meditate on it, then it is sin. (See Mathew 5:28.)

No matter how holy you may be or how long you have been a Christian, from time to time Satan will attack you. His end is coming, and he knows it. Until then he is roaming about "as a roaring lion...seeking whom he may devour" (1 Pet. 5:8).

The Bible says "as a roaring lion." It does not say he is a roaring lion; he simply wears that disguise. If you are filled with the Word, you will find that the roaring lion is toothless and has no power over you! You cannot stop the devil from putting a thought into your head any more than you can stop a bird from flying over your head. It's just one of those things that happens. As long as you are here on Earth, there will be interference. But we can stop the devil from building strongholds in our minds by casting out those thoughts. We must bring the *psuche* man in line with the Spirit. We must bring our spirit and soul together and grow in power to dominate the flesh and the body. We must learn how to get the *psuche* man trained to the point where he can walk in harmony with our spirit.

Romans 12:1 says, "I beseech you therefore, brethren, by the mercies of God, that ye present your bodies a living sacrifice, holy, acceptable unto God, which is your reasonable service." Another translation reads, "...which is your spiritual service of worship." In other words, you present your body to God as a living sacrifice.

God Does Not Control Your Thoughts

As believers in Christ our bodies are the temple of the Holy Spirit, and we ought to be Spirit-controlled. We ought not be ruled by the appetites of the world and the appetites of the *psuche* man. Our spirit is always seeking after God and desires to do the right thing. You do not have to be concerned that your spirit is going against God, because if you are a child of God your spirit will always be looking toward God. The Bible says you have been recreated on the inside. You have been made the righteousness of God in Christ. Yet, although our spirit desires to do what is right, we do things we wish we had not done.

God says for us to present the body as a living sacrifice, but that is very difficult unless the spirit is in control. If the body and the soul are in control, we cannot be a living sacrifice.

David said, "My soul longeth, yea, even fainteth for the courts of the Lord" (Ps. 84:2). David could get so thrilled in his worship of the Lord that his soul wanted to be present in the throne room of God.

We can get to the place where our soul cries out for God. We only get there by learning how to get the *psuche* man under control and letting the spirit and the soul get the body in order. The body is not an evil thing. God created it to be a holy thing. Neither are the soul, the mind, the will and the emotions evil things. The problem is that the soul has been programmed with ungodly thoughts.

The mind is a computer. It can only spit out what is put into it. When you were not a Christian, or when you became a Christian but were ignorant of the Word of God, your mind was programmed by the world. Every time a situation arises, your mind instantly wants to react the world's way rather than God's way. This programming needs to be changed. Paul discusses this in Romans 12:2. "And be not conformed to this world: but be ye transformed by the renewing of your mind, that ye may prove what is that good, and acceptable, and perfect, will of God."

If you want to do the will of God, your mind has to be transformed. Your *psuche* man has to be transformed. The soul has to be changed.

The mind has tremendous storage capacity. Because of sin, very few people ever attain the full, God-given capability of their minds.

Adam had a tremendous mind. The Bible says he named all the animals, all the species. It does not say that God gave him the names. It says he named them. Think of all the animals there are, all the different subgroups, all the different genuses, species and families, and you will realize it had to take tremendous mental power to accomplish that task. Just the act of naming everything was a creative power from God. God intended for all of us to have that power. Because of the dominion of sin, Satan took control of the world. When man fell, he lost a good bit of that mind power as

God intended for it to be used. Before you became a Christian, your mind was constantly assaulted with the spirit of the world. Even after you became a Christian, if you did not immediately begin to renew your mind it was still assaulted by the world's system and the activities of the enemy. As long as you are on earth your soul will be susceptible to counter-programming from the enemy.

We have to reprogram our minds. Reprogramming forces out the old programming. The Bible says we must be transformed by the renewing of our minds. We must put in a new database so that we can draw off of it and act according to it instead of what has been there in the past. The enemy will still try to input his own thoughts. He will constantly come, as the Bible says, as one who sows tares among the wheat. Even when you are sowing good seed and getting your mind renewed, the devil will try to sow weeds to interrupt your programming.

Realize that transformation is a process and not an instantaneous change.

If You Are Not in Control of Your Thoughts, Who Is?

Now that we know our minds must be renewed, we need to find out how it is accomplished. God never asks us to do anything without providing what we need to accomplish the task.

Second Corinthians 10:3-5 says, "For though we walk in the flesh, we do not war after the flesh: (For the weapons of our warfare are not carnal, but mighty through God to the pulling down of strong holds;). Casting down imaginations, and every high thing that exalteth itself against the knowledge of God, and bringing into captivity every thought to the obedience of Christ."

In the spiritual battle for the mind, our first task is tearing down strongholds. When it seems you have almost no control over your thought processes or actions, a stronghold exists in your life. You have control, but it may seem as though you do not.

Strongholds take root because we have meditated on the word of the enemy. Once a stronghold is in place, our minds think automatically in that direction.

Fear is the opposite of faith. Fear works as a catalyst in the kingdom of the enemy just as faith works as a catalyst in the kingdom of God. Faith unlocks the blessings of God. Faith brings God's power to bear on our lives. Fear brings Satan's power to bear on our lives. The Bible differentiates between fear and reverence. Reverence is respect. A natural reverence is built into all human beings, a respect for things that will harm them. God has placed that inside us. Sometimes people's natural reverence or respect becomes unreasoning fear. Unreasoning fear is based on an illogical premise.

I ministered to a lady who had such a problem with unreasoning fear that she could not drive her car. She would reach the middle of an intersection and be so afraid an accident would happen that she would turn off her car, get out and have to leave it there. I can tell you she was not popular with other motorists.

I ministered to another woman who had just bought a new car and could not drive it because she had a fear of plastic. When she sat in the car, she smelled new plastic, and she thought the plastic fumes were going to hurt her. That is unreasoning fear. It is from the devil.

Satan forms strongholds in people's minds. Suppose someone has a stomach pain. The first thing the devil does is flip up a flash card: INDIGESTION. Then the person says, "No. Too painful for indigestion. It has to be something else." The next flash card says: HERNIA. The person says, "No, no. I just had a checkup the other day. I cannot have a hernia. I got a clean bill of health on that." The next thing that flashes up is: APPENDICITIS. "No, no, it's in the wrong place." Finally the devil flashes up: STOMACH CANCER. "Oh! I knew that was it! That's what Uncle Joe died of!" The person develops an unreasoning fear. Fear makes a place for that sickness to enter in. Fear opens the door to the devil.

When unreasoning fear enters in, it forms a stronghold in the mind. Once a stronghold is established, a person becomes a prisoner of that stronghold and always reacts according to the stronghold rather than the will of God.

God never created men to relate to a spirit of fear. "For God hath not given us the spirit of fear; but of power, and of love, and of a sound mind" (2 Tim. 1:7).

We ought to be able to face anything in life without unreasoning fear. However, there is no such thing as facing danger without giving due consideration to the circumstances. People of great courage consider all angles of a situation before they do what must be done. This is natural respect that God has placed within us. It is what sets believers who know the Word apart from other believers. They have separated themselves from the fear of man and move ahead into whatever God has prepared for them.

If unreasoning fear keeps you from doing what God has called you to do, you will not succeed. You must be free from unreasoning fear to succeed.

Strongholds are built up in the mind, and that is where they must be dealt with. Did you know Satan cannot use anything to tempt us except those things which are common to man? He must use such things as lust of the flesh, the pride of life and so forth. However, God says the weapons of our warfare are not carnal but divinely powerful through God to the pulling down of strongholds. We are not limited to *psuche* ability and knowledge in renewing the mind.

God's power always overcomes the power of the enemy. When you apply the power of the Word to your mind, strongholds must capitulate. They must give up their hold no matter how long they have been there. You apply the power of God through the Word of God.

The first step to renewing your mind and becoming free from strongholds is to cast down imaginations. How do we cast down an imagination? An imagination is any thought contrary to God's

Word, bringing fear and bondage. Therefore we must attack that thought or imagination and cast it out. We can simply say, "Thought, or Satan (or whatever spirit it is), I rebuke you in the name of Jesus. I command you to depart from my mind. I will not fellowship with you." You may also take hold of the sword of the Spirit, which is the Word of God. Speak the Word of God to counteract the thought.

For example, if fear is lodged in your mind, you could say, "Fear, in Jesus' name, I take authority over you. You cannot remain in me because God has not given me a spirit of fear, but of love, power and a sound mind."

We cast out thoughts most effectively by attacking them with the Word of God. We are not trying to wipe our minds clean, but we are trying to reprogram them with the Word of God. We cast down imaginations with the Word of God. That is a weapon of our warfare.

We can make our thoughts obedient to Christ only when the Word is active in our lives. Jesus Christ Himself is the Word of God. We have to program our minds in line with God's Word. Memorization by itself will do you no good. When we speak the Word of God and hear the Word of God, our minds are reprogrammed. Romans 10:17 says, "So then faith cometh by hearing, and hearing by the word of God."

When we hear the Word of God, it goes down into our spirits. Revelation knowledge comes from our spirit, and that knowledge is played upon our minds. When we want our minds to be renewed in a certain area, we must search out all the scriptures we can find relating to that particular area. Whether it is fear of some type, financial lack, an attitude of poverty or anything else, search the Word and see what it says. Go after that stronghold, and renew your mind. Speak the Word. Confess the Word of God out of your mouth, for out of the abundance of the heart the mouth speaks.

The more of the Word you store in your spirit, the more it comes out of your mouth. The more of the Word that comes out of your mouth, the more that goes in. You develop a cycle that is the best perpetual motion machine ever invented. When you speak the Word, you build faith and receive the blessing, which causes you to speak more of the Word, which builds stronger faith, which begets more blessing. Keep that going, and your mind will be renewed.

To fulfill the will of God in your life, your mind must be renewed. The *psuche* man must be renewed so that your mind can walk hand in hand with your spirit to bring the body into submission. Speaking the Word of God to your body will actually cause it to come in line with your spirit, which always seeks after righteousness.

If the soul and spirit are at war, one cannot accomplish much for the kingdom of God because precious effort is wasted on an interior battle rather than promoting the things of God.

CHAPTER TEN

New Covenant Living

We know that the word *psuche* refers to natural life, soul or mind. These three work together interchangeably. In this chapter we will find out how important it is to reprogram our minds. We will review Scripture and examine the life of an individual who had an unrenewed mind and learn what happened after his mind was renewed.

Galatians 5:16 says, "This I say then, Walk in the Spirit, and ye shall not fulfill the lust of the flesh." Most people approach walking in the Spirit backward. They say, "Don't commit the lust of the flesh, and then you will walk in the Spirit." That is not what the Bible says. The Bible says, "Walk in the Spirit, and ye shall not fulfill the lust of the flesh."

Scripture states this for a specific purpose. When we renew our minds with the Word, the spirit joins together with the soul; together these two are able to rule over the desires of the flesh. We will never achieve victory over the flesh simply by disciplining it. We must walk in the Spirit. As we listen to God, renew our minds by the Word and join the spirit with the soul, the flesh will come into line automatically.

If the soul and the flesh join together (two are stronger than one), they will overcome the spirit and we will not be able to live the way God wants us to live. On the other hand, if the spirit and the soul work together, they can take control over the flesh. The flesh will come into line with the Word of God, and this change will be evident in our actions. However, we cannot simply discipline the flesh and expect to become spiritual. It doesn't work that way. Disciplining the flesh only inflames the appetites.

Galatians 5:17 says, "For the flesh lusteth against the Spirit, and the Spirit against the flesh: and these are contrary the one to the other: so that ye cannot do the things that ye would."

Did you know that your physical body can become accustomed to sin just as it becomes accustomed to righteousness?

"But if ye be led of the Spirit, ye are not under the law. Now the works of the flesh are manifest, which are these; Adultery, fornication, uncleanness, lasciviousness, idolatry, witchcraft, hatred, variance, emulations, wrath, strife, seditions, heresies, envyings, murders, drunkenness, revellings, and such like: of the which I tell you before, as I have also told you in time past, that they which do such things shall not inherit the kingdom of God. But the fruit of the Spirit is love, joy, peace, longsuffering, gentleness, goodness, faith, meekness, temperance: against such there is no law" (vv. 18-23).

We have seen what the flesh produces and what the Spirit of God produces. If the soul and the flesh gang up on the spirit, these fleshly things will be manifested in your life. However, if the Spirit is in control and your mind is renewed, your life will be filled with the peace of God and the fruit of the Spirit.

"And they that are Christ's have crucified the flesh with the affections and lusts. If we live in the Spirit, let us also walk in the Spirit" (vv. 24-25).

Living in the Abundance

God is calling us to be Spirit-conscious! Remember that the spirit realm has been here far longer than the realm of the natural. When everything in the natural realm is gone, the spirit will still be there. The spirit realm is the ultimate reality.

People who get involved in spiritualism and converse with familiar spirits are seeking spiritual power. They realize the spirit world is far more powerful and far more real than the natural world, but they are seeking power from the wrong side of the spirit realm. Man desires the supernatural because he was created supernaturally. Because we are spirits dwelling in physical bodies, we will always long to contact that realm from which we were created. It is a natural law that exists in the earth. God created us as spirits and clothed us in flesh. There is coming a time, of course, when our bodies will be changed. Then the spirit world will be as real to us as the paper on which these words are printed. When, as the Bible says, this mortality shall put on immortality, all of our spiritual senses will be activated.

The spirit man has senses just as the physical man does. The Bible says, "Taste and see that the Lord is good." This we do with the sense of the spirit.

The prayers of the saints go up to God as a sweet-smelling savor. We become spirit-conscious by learning the Word of God. When we feed our spirit's with the Word of God, we nourish our spirits and become even more accustomed to flowing in the things of the Spirit.

If we try to flow in the things of the Spirit apart from the Word, we end up with a distorted idea of what ought to happen. Many Christians get excited about moving in the gifts of the Spirit. They seek the experiences themselves. Seeking the experiences apart from the Word opens the door to manifestations that can come from any spirit and not just God's Spirit.

Let's look at the life of Paul and the battles he fought to renew his mind. Even though he had tremendous revelation knowledge from God, he also had tremendous struggles with the flesh. He overcame them through the Spirit, but every once in a while he made a mistake. He was always quick to repent and do what was right.

First let's see what Paul, or Saul, was like before his conversion. Acts 7 tells the story of the martyrdom of Stephen. Stephen had preached the Word of God and done great signs and wonders among the people. They brought him before the counsel; that did not stop his boldness. He told them they had killed the Messiah. This did not go over too well with the Jewish leaders. They hired some people to bear false witness against him and accuse him of blasphemy, condemning him to die.

Acts 7:57-58 says, "Then they cried out with a loud voice, and stopped their ears, and ran upon him with one accord, and cast him out of the city, and stoned him: and the witnesses laid down their clothes at a young man's feet, whose name was Saul."

Saul is the same individual who later (as Paul) won thousands of people to the Lord. He was the one who controlled his life to the point where he could say, "I decide whether I'm staying on this earth or whether I'm going. No man will take my life from me. I don't know if it is better for me to stay here with you or go and be with the Lord, but because now I think it is better to be with you, I'm going to stay."

We find Paul in his unregenerate state participating in the murder of Stephen. He was a member of the ruling counsel. He had the best education the Jews had to offer. Even though he did not directly participate in the stoning, the Bible says he held cloaks. In legal language today we would call him an accessory to the crime. He aided and abetted those who murdered Stephen.

"And they stoned Stephen, calling upon God, and saying, Lord Jesus, receive my spirit. And he kneeled down, and cried with a loud voice, Lord, lay not this sin to their charge. And when he had said this, he fell asleep" (vv. 59-60).

Acts 8:1-4 says, "And Saul was consenting unto his death. And at that time there was a great persecution against the church which was at Jerusalem; and they were all scattered abroad throughout the regions of Judaea and Samaria, except the apostles. And devout men carried Stephen to his burial, and made great lamentation over him. As for Saul, he made havoc of the church, entering into every house, and haling men and women committed them to prison. Therefore they that were scattered abroad went every where preaching the word."

Acts 9:1-2 says, "And Saul, yet breathing out threatenings and slaughter against the disciples of the Lord, went unto the high priest, And desired of him letters to Damascus to the synagogues, that if he found any of this way, whether they were men or women, he might bring them bound unto Jerusalem." Saul had access to the high priest, which indicates his authority and position in Israel. Why did he go to the high priest? He wanted letters recommending him to the authorities at Damascus. He wanted to get some more Christians. It wasn't enough that he was wreaking havoc in the church at Jerusalem. He decided to take his own personal crusade to Damascus and deal with the Christians there as well.

However, God had other plans for Saul.

Translated from Darkness to Light

"And as he journeyed, he came near Damascus: and suddenly there shined round about him a light from heaven: And he fell to the earth, and heard a voice saying unto him, Saul, Saul, why persecutest thou me? And he said, Who art thou, Lord? And the Lord said, I am Jesus whom thou persecutest: it is hard for thee to kick against the pricks" (vv. 3-5).

Literally Jesus was saying this: "I have called you. It is impossible for you to escape the ministry I have planned for you. If you resist, it is only going to hurt you more." Many people are dragged kicking and screaming into the will of God. In fact, some people leave two black heel marks as they enter the kingdom of heaven. It ought not be this way.

Saul actually thought he was doing right in persecuting the Christians. These people who were preaching Jesus as Messiah were not following the traditions of the elders. They were not following the written law or the oral law. Of course, Saul was a Pharisee, and we know what the Pharisees were like. Jesus called them a brood of vipers. He said they were children of the devil. They were very religious in every way except one: They did not know God at all. Their understanding was based upon the traditions of men.

Saul, of course, was converted and came into the saving knowledge of the Lord Jesus Christ. When he was converted, the part of him that was changed was his spirit, not his mind or the psuche man. When we are born again, something happens on the inside. The mind is not wiped out; we do not forget everything we know. All that programming is still there. Paul was aware of this. Look at what he had to say about himself much later in his ministry.

"And I thank Christ Jesus our Lord, who hath enabled me, for that he counted me faithful, putting me into the ministry; who was before a blasphemer, and a persecutor, and injurious: but I obtained mercy, because I did it ignorantly in unbelief" (1 Tim. 1:12-13).

What Paul was saying is, "In my unbelief, I did not believe in the Word of God." Unbelief does not mean you do not know something. Unbelief means you know and yet give allegiance to things other than the Word of God. Any belief system not based on the Word is unbelief. In other words, what we do that is based on God's Word translates as belief in God. If a belief system is based on man's ideas and feelings, it is unbelief. This is the kind of situation in which Paul found himself. He knew the rules and regulations of the Pharisees. He persecuted Jesus because of those traditions. But he said, "God gave me mercy because I did those things ignorantly in unbelief." In other words, "My mind, the *psuche* part of me, was trained in that area. That was all I knew. I did it ignorantly, not on purpose. That was the way I was educated."

"And the grace of our Lord was exceeding abundant with faith and love which is in Christ Jesus. This is a faithful saying, and worthy of all acceptation, that Christ Jesus came into the world to save sinners; of whom I am chief" (vv. 14-15).

Paul openly declared himself the worst of all sinners. Yet he knew he had been made the righteousness of God in Christ Jesus, because he had written about that several letters earlier. He was simply pointing out that in dealing with the *psuche* man, he still had struggles.

No matter how holy we get, we will never attain full perfection until the day we are changed. This does not mean we shouldn't strive for perfection. We should look forward to going days, weeks, months and years without committing sin. The point is, you will never get that way unless you start now. Paul had to deal with his mind, his soul (his *psuche* man) just as you and I must.

Romans 6:12 says, "Let not sin therefore reign in your mortal body, that ye should obey it in the lusts thereof." Remember, your body becomes accustomed to certain appetites and activities. God wants our bodies to obey what we know in our spirit to be true in the Word. The body, having certain appetites, wields power. If we do not know how to deal with it, the body will drive us to do the works of the flesh that we read about in Galatians 5.

"Neither yield ye your members as instruments of unrighteousness unto sin: but yield yourselves unto God, as those that are alive from the dead, and your members as instruments of righteousness unto God" (v. 13).

God desires that your body, every part of your body, be yielded to Him as an instrument of righteousness. Everything you do with your body ought to glorify God, whether it's playing sports, singing for the Lord or laying hands on the sick. If you do things with your body that are not glorifying to God, it is sin and therefore allows destruction to be at work in your members.

"For sin shall not have dominion over you: for ye are not under the law, but under grace. What then? shall we sin, because we are not under the law, but under grace? God forbid" (vv. 14-15). Many people, when they find out they are not under the law, become lackadaisical about sin and say, "We can do whatever we want to do. After all, we are not bound by this commandment or that commandment anymore." When you preach grace, you have a lot of religious people who come to you and say, "You're just giving people a license to sin. If you tell them they are not under the law, they'll just go out and do whatever they want." People will sin whether they have a license to or not. The point is, as Christians we are no longer bound to a set of rigid rules that God gave under the old covenant. We are new-covenant people. God said we would no longer be bound to the written law, the ten commandments, but that a new law would be written upon our hearts.

The old covenant law existed because people were not born again. They had to have a written law before them as a constant reminder not to sin. We have a new law written upon our hearts, upon our spirits, because we have been born again by the Spirit of God. The Word of God, Jesus Christ, lives inside us. We already have knowledge of what is right and wrong. We do not have to go to some dusty parchment to see if it is right or wrong. We have an intuitive sense, as Christians, about what things are right and what things are wrong. It is called the witness of the Spirit. God has taken that new law and written it upon our hearts.

Jesus said there are two commandments we must obey. First, love God with all your heart, soul, mind and strength. Second, love your neighbor as yourself. Paul wrote in Galatians 5, "It will perform all the law, if you love your neighbor as yourself" (see v.

144

14). A new law has been written on our hearts, not a volume of rules that have to be followed, but a new law, the law of love. The love of God has been shed abroad into our hearts by the Holy Spirit.

If we operate in the law of love we will fulfill all of God's law, even the written law. The Jews had to carry the law around. Have you ever noticed in the New Testament the word *phylacteries*? Jesus spoke against the Pharisees because they were broadening their phylacteries. Phylacteries were little boxes in which they carried around the law of God, or the Ten Commandments, and all the things they had to remember. These little boxes were bound on their wrists or foreheads, or sometimes their chests, depending on how much they had with them. The Pharisees were making their phylacteries bigger so everyone would think they were more religious. In other words, they carried more Scripture around with them.

Today some people carry around twenty-pound Bibles. When they go witnessing, they bring along a little red wagon to tote their Bible. Everyone knows these people are strange. It is much more sensible to carry a pocket New Testament so you do not immediately put people on the defensive.

The tradition of carrying the law of God started in a good way, because the Jews had to remember the laws to do what God commanded them. But Jesus came and said, "I will write a new law on your heart, and when I do you won't have to worry about all the other commandments because you will naturally accomplish them."

The Pharisees took what God had given as good and worked the systems of men into it, causing it to bring bondage. Jesus devotes a whole chapter in the book of Matthew to the scribes and Pharisees and their various activities.

Romans 6 says, "Know ye not, that to whom ye yield yourselves servants to obey, his servants ye are to whom ye obey; whether of sin unto death, or of obedience unto righteousness?" (v. 16). If you yield yourself to sin, eventually it will control you. If you yield yourself to the Spirit of God, you will bring yourself into the light, and the Spirit will guide and direct you.

"But God be thanked, that ye were the servants of sin, but ye have obeyed from the heart that form of doctrine which was delivered you. Being then made free from sin, ye became the servants of righteousness. I speak after the manner of men because of the infirmity of your flesh: for as ye have yielded your members servants to uncleanness and to iniquity unto iniquity; even so now yield your members servants to righteousness unto holiness" (vv. 17-19).

Paul wrote this to the Romans because they still had difficulty with the flesh. Even though they were made the righteousness of Christ on the inside, they still had trouble. He was exhorting them to become more conscious of the righteousness that dwelt in them rather than the unrighteousness that was at work in their flesh.

"For when ye were the servants of sin, ye were free from righteousness" (v. 20). When an individual is a servant of sin, his consciousness is not disturbed by righteousness.

"What fruit had ye then in those things whereof ye are now ashamed? for the end of those things is death" (v. 21). He is saying, "Why do you want to go back to the way things were? What did that profit you? What fruit did you have there?" We know what fruit they had. It can be found at the end of the chapter.

"But now being made free from sin, and become servants to God, ye have your fruit unto holiness, and the end everlasting life. For the wages of sin is death; but the gift of God is eternal life through Jesus Christ our Lord" (vv. 22-23).

If we serve God in righteousness we will live in freedom, happiness and peace. If we operate in sin, and the flesh and the *psuche* man work together, life will be very miserable for believers.

It is not necessary, according to God's Word, for people to confess every sin they can think of before coming to know Jesus as Lord. God does say we need to repent. But this is what the Bible says we need to do to be saved: "That if thou shalt confess with thy mouth the Lord Jesus, and shalt believe in thine heart that God hath raised him from the dead, thou shalt be saved. For with the heart man believeth unto righteousness; and with the mouth confession is made unto salvation" (Rom. 10:9-10).

We do not need to browbeat people and tell them they are sinners. They know it already. If the first thing you say to a person is, "You're a sinner and you need to repent," you put him on the defensive so that you cannot get through with the Word of God. Rather, preach the Word of God to him. Tell him Jesus loves him and that he can enter into a relationship with Him by receiving Him as Lord and believing in his heart that God raised Him from the dead.

Did you know there are no atheists in foxholes? It is easy to be an atheist when the pressure is not on. But when the pressure is turned on, even the atheist starts looking for God. When the shells start flying, everyone starts praying, and sin is obvious to all. Romans 7:1, 5-6 says, "Know ye not, brethren, (for I speak to them that know the law,) how that the law hath dominion over a man as long as he liveth?...For when we were in the flesh, the motions of sins, which were by the law, did work in our members to bring forth fruit unto death. But now we are delivered from the law...." We have been set free from the bondage of the law. "...That being dead wherein we were held; that we should serve in newness of spirit, and not in the oldness of the letter" (v. 6).

Remember that the law was given for people who were separated from God. Now that our spirits have been made alive unto Christ Jesus, we have a relationship with Him, Spirit to spirit. We serve Him in newness of spirit, and not in the oldness of the letter of the law.

"What shall we say then? Is the law sin? God forbid." The law is not a bad thing. God gave the law for a specific reason. "Nay, I had not known sin, but by the law: for I had not known lust, except the law had said, Thou shalt not covet" (v. 7). Paul had no knowledge of sin until knowledge of the commandment came. The commandment pointed out the difference between right and wrong. Do you remember what happened to Adam and Eve?

God told Adam and Eve not to eat of the tree of knowledge of good and evil, for when they ate of it, they would die. Why? Because when knowledge of the commandment comes, the idea of sin begins to take form. When you have knowledge only about that which is good, you are motivated to do that which is good. But when you develop knowledge of that which is evil, you are enticed to do things which are evil.

"But sin, taking occasion by the commandment, wrought in me all manner of concupiscence [evil or lusting]. For without the law sin was dead" (v. 8). When the knowledge of the commandment came, sin took advantage of me because I knew that something was wrong. The Ten Commandments say, "Thou shalt not murder." Knowledge of that commandment allows us to make a choice. We are either going to do evil or we are going to do good. It is the knowledge of the commandment that gives us that choice. The possibility of murder has always existed, but knowledge of the commandment gives the opportunity for sin. That is why grace is so much better. While we were under the law, the law was a constant reminder that there was evil out there. When we are under grace, we have a constant reminder of God and His holiness and our relationship to Him—not our separation from Him by the law.

"For I was alive without the law once: but when the commandment came, sin revived, and I died" (v. 9). There was a time in Paul's life when he did not have knowledge of the law. The Bible says that he was alive. But then knowledge of the commandment came, and sin revived, and he fell, or died. When children are born into this world, they do not have the knowledge of good and evil. They do not know the difference between right and wrong. At whatever point a child understands the commandments of right and wrong, that is when sin takes occasion and they fall. They lose the innocence they had. Jesus always wanted little children to come to Him because they were pure and innocent. Children who die before they have a knowledge of the commandment do not go to hell; they go to heaven. Knowledge of the commandment must come in order for us to be separated from God.

When a person receives the knowledge of the commandment, sin takes the opportunity to come in and say, thou shalt not do this. What do you start thinking about? Exactly what you should not do. As you think, so you will become. If you think about what you should not do all the time, you will be constantly reminded about that thing and tempted to do it. That is why Jesus did not come with "Thou shalt nots." His words were affirmative: "Love God, and love your neighbor as yourself." If you do these things, you won't have problems with anything else. Rather than focusing on things that are negative, you are looking to Jesus Christ and walking in the law of love, which is positive. The law of love allows us to overcome all sin by separating ourselves from it.

"For we know that the law is spiritual. But I am carnal [or natural], sold under sin. For that which I do I allow not: for what I would, that do I not; but what I hate, that do I" (vv. 14-15). Paul is saying, "The things that I don't want to do, I'm doing. The things that I want to do, I'm not doing. The very thing that I hate the most, I'm doing anyway."

Here is an anointed servant of God who has revelation knowledge, and yet he is saying, "I'm having the same trouble that you have."

"If then I do that which I would not, I consent unto the law that it is good" (v. 16). He knows that the law points out righteousness and unrighteousness. If he does something wrong, he can't blame the law. It is his own choice. He knows that the law is righteous, but if he does that which is wrong, it is his own responsibility.

"Now then it is no more I that do it..." Listen to the difference here. When he says "I," he means the born-again Paul, the recreated spirit, in which there dwells no evil. He says, "Now then it is no more I that do it, but sin that dwelleth in me" (v. 17). It is not the spirit but the unprogrammed *psuche* man that is still influenced by a sinful pattern. "For I know that in me" [he makes the differentiation here so it's real important] "For I know that in me (that is, in my flesh,) dwelleth no good thing: for to will is present with me; but how to perform that which is good I find not" (v. 18). In other words, he is saying, "On the inside of me the will is there to do good. My spirit is always ready to do God's will, but how to perform that which is good I find not, or, I know not."

Romans 7:19-23 says, "For the good that I would I do not: but the evil which I would not, that I do. Now if I do that I would not, it is no more I that do it, but sin that dwelleth in me. I find then a law, that, when I would do good, evil is present with me [or appetites of the flesh]. For I delight in the law of God after the inward man: But I see another law in my members, warring against the law of my mind, and bringing me into captivity to the law of sin which is in my members."

Verse 24 says, "O wretched man that I am! who shall deliver me from the body of this death?" Here he was, the top minister in the world, still having problems with the flesh. Even though we may be tremendously anointed by the power of God and have understanding of the Word, it does not mean we have arrived. Our minds still need to be renewed, and our flesh still must be controlled. It is a day-by-day battle. We are transformed daily by the renewing of the mind.

Paul then says, "Who is going to help me? Who is going to deliver me from the body of this death?"

"I thank God through Jesus Christ our Lord. So then with the mind I myself serve the law of God; but with the flesh the law of sin" (v. 25).

He is saying, "I am renewing my mind. I am working with my mind to serve the law of God, but I know the flesh serves the law of sin."

Finally Paul comes to a tremendous revelation, found in Romans 8:1-2. It is important to note that in the original Greek there are no chapters, no punctuation. Many people read chapter 7 and get depressed; they never go on and read chapter 8.

"There is therefore now no condemnation to them which are in Christ Jesus, who walk not after the flesh, but after the Spirit" (8:1). "If we walk in the Spirit, we will not fulfill the lust of the flesh." Paul was saying, "Even though all these negative things may happen and we may fall away several times a day, Jesus says, 'There is no condemnation added unto you. God is not looking at you, judging you, if your purpose is to walk according to the Spirit, because He knows there is a battle going on.'" When a mistake is made or sin is carried out, that is not the time to run away from God; that is the time to go to God and repent.

In 1 John 1:9 it says, "If we confess our sins, he is faithful and just to forgive us our sins, and to cleanse us from all unrighteousness." We must confess sin immediately and not let it control us.

"For the law of the Spirit of life in Christ Jesus hath made me free from the law of sin and death" (Rom. 8:2). There is a higher law than the law of sin and death: It is the law of the Spirit of life that God has given in Christ Jesus. When we are sensitive to Him and begin to walk in the Spirit, we will not fulfill those things that are the lusts of the flesh.

Galatians 5:14 says, "For all the law is fulfilled in one word, even in this; Thou shalt love thy neighbor as thyself." Love is the law of the Spirit of life in Christ Jesus. If we love our neighbors as ourselves, then we will be able to do what is necessary.

The *psuche* man must be changed and the mind renewed. "Be ye transformed by the renewing of your mind." We have to take authority over those strongholds that have existed in our minds, so that our minds will be built up. Then, with the spirit and the mind working together, the flesh will come in line with the Word of God.

Strongholds can be positive or negative. When Satan puts something in our mind and builds a stronghold, that thing controls us, driving us to do evil. But the Bible says the Word of the Lord is a strong tower, and the righteous run to it and are safe.

It is possible to build positive strongholds in our minds by renewing our minds to the Word. Once that godly stronghold is there, it is impossible for the devil to assail it. Even as we were under the bondage of negative strongholds in the past that caused us to do evil things without thinking, so we will begin to do righteous things naturally. It is a total changeover from the old system of the flesh to a new system of the Spirit. God desires that we be blessed and that the life of God flow through us, as we think on good and positive things (see Phil. 4:8).

CHAPTER ELEVEN

Be Filled with The Spirit

In this chapter we will discuss the laying on of hands and the baptism of the Holy Spirit. Realize that when we lay our hands on individuals, the spirit that is upon us or upon them can be transferred back and forth. When we pray for someone for the baptism of the Holy Spirit, it is important that we lay hands on them. However, an individual can receive the baptism of the Holy Spirit without having hands laid on them.

No one laid hands on me when I received the baptism of the Holy Spirit. I was just walking around the front yard one night and decided I wanted to receive the baptism of the Holy Spirit. So I did. I prayed and asked God to honor His Word. I began to speak in tongues. No one laid hands on me. However, when we are praying for people to receive the baptism, we should certainly use the tools that God has given us.

One of these tools is the laying on of hands, given to us so that we can impart all that God has blessed us with, and so that others can also receive God's blessings.

In Acts 8 there is a big "revival" going on in Samaria. Philip, one of the original deacons, had gone to Samaria from Jerusalem. Samaria was considered an evil place by the Jews because it was originally the capital of the northern kingdom. At the close of King Solomon's reign, all of Israel was united. Solomon's son Rehoboam, not being as wise as Solomon, aggravated some of the children of Israel. As a result, ten tribes separated and formed their own kingdom under a king named Jeroboam. Among the tribes that left the control of Rehoboam were Judah and Benjamin. Then there were two kingdoms, the kingdom of Judah and the kingdom of Israel.

Israel's capital city was Samaria. The Samaritans were rebellious to God. They had intermarried with people who were not Jews. To the Pharisees, the Samaritans were unclean and considered unacceptable people with whom to fellowship. Jesus Himself told the story of the Good Samaritan. He even had a discussion with a woman who was from Samaria. She was the woman at the well.

Philip was known as Philip the Evangelist. He had gone to Samaria to preach the Word. People were getting healed, delivered and saved. Tremendous things were happening by the power of God. Some of those things had to do with the laying on of hands. Then Peter and John came down to Samaria. Let's look at what the Word says beginning at Acts 8:14.

"Now when the apostles which were at Jerusalem heard that Samaria had received the word of God, they sent unto them Peter and John: Who, when they were come down, prayed for them, that they might receive the Holy Ghost: (For as yet he was fallen upon none of them: only they were baptized in the name of the Lord Jesus)" (vv. 14-16).

Even though they had received repentance from their sins and had been delivered, they had not been baptized or received the baptism of the Holy Spirit.

Verse 17 is the key verse: "Then laid they their hands on them, and they received the Holy Ghost."

The baptism of the Holy Spirit may be received in several ways. An individual can pray in accordance with Luke 11:13 and receive the baptism of the Holy Spirit by faith. God gives the Holy Spirit to those who ask Him. An individual may receive the Holy Spirit through the laying on of hands without having even asked for the baptism of the Holy Spirit. Or an individual may ask and we may lay hands on him. There are times when the anointing of God is such that you can simply lay hands on people and pray for them and they will receive the Holy Spirit.

Whenever possible it should be explained to people how to receive the Holy Spirit so they will not have questions later. I have been in services where I planned to explain how to receive the baptism of the Holy Spirit, and when I came near the people, they just fell on the floor and spoke in other tongues. There isn't too much to say when that happens.

In any case, we find that the Holy Spirit was moving through the laying on of the apostles' hands, and people were receiving the Holy Spirit.

God Will Never Lead You Where His Spirit Cannot Keep You

The Spirit of God is actually transferred through the person ministering by the point of contact (the laying on of hands). The nine gifts of the Spirit cannot be possessed. Rather, we are vessels through which they move. The gifts of tongues, interpretation, prophecy, word of wisdom, word of knowledge, healing, miracles, distinguishing of spirits and faith are for the people to receive. These gifts move through us as the Holy Spirit wills and according to whether we are appropriate vessels for those gifts to move through.

When we lay hands on someone and a gift of healing is moving through us, that gift of healing is transmitted through our hands to that individual. The same happens with the Holy Spirit. When we are praying for someone to receive the Holy Spirit, we lay hands on them and the anointing is transferred to the individual so that they receive the baptism of the Holy Spirit and begin to speak in other tongues.

This particular scripture shows us that when the hands were laid on, the people received the Holy Ghost not just in statement but in action.

There was a certain individual named Simon, who was a magician. Verse 13 says, "Then Simon himself believed also: and when he was baptized, he continued with Philip, and wondered, beholding the miracles and signs which were done."

Verse 9 tells us who Simon was. "But there was a certain man, called Simon, which beforetime in the same city used sorcery, and bewitched the people of Samaria, giving out that himself was some great one." After following and observing all that had been done by Philip, Simon received Jesus as his Lord.

The reason we know the Holy Spirit was given when the apostles laid their hands on these individuals is because there was evidence of the baptism (see Acts 2). The people began to speak with other tongues as the Spirit gave them utterance.

Verse 18 says, "And when Simon saw that through laying on of the apostles' hands the Holy Ghost was given, he offered them money." Some kind of power was imparted to them when hands were laid on. There had to be some kind of outward sign or manifestation in order for Simon to see something.

It would be one thing if the Word said, "And Simon believed that the Holy Ghost was given when the apostles' hands were laid on him." That would be a statement of faith indicating his own personal experience with God. But Simon saw some kind of physical manifestation that attracted his attention. It could have been several things.

"...Saying, Give me also this power, that on whomsoever I lay hands, he may receive the Holy Ghost" (v. 19). As a magician, Simon was intimately acquainted with the practice of laying on hands. It has been going on for a long time and is even practiced in pagan rituals, witchcraft and sorcery.

Simon understood that power was being transferred, and he wanted the same power so that when he laid hands on people they could receive the Holy Ghost. He even offered money for it. Peter told him, "Thy money perish with thee, because thou hast thought that the gift of God may be purchased with money" (v. 20). Then he asked him to repent.

Verse 24 says, "Then answered Simon, and said, Pray ye to the Lord for me, that none of these things which ye have spoken come upon me." He became concerned, since his bad attitude had been exposed.

If someone has not received the baptism of the Holy Spirit and is perhaps questioning whether it is real even while desiring it, his faith level is not too high, is it?

When an individual's faith level is not very high, he may have already asked God for the Holy Spirit and nothing happened. God desires to reach this individual, but there is unbelief in the way.

Such a person has not been able to receive the Holy Spirit on his own, so he needs help. When we lay hands on him, we become channels through which the power of God moves.

Let me tell you how this works. Many of you are aware that television stations have a certain range, depending upon their power. That is why there are microwave relay towers in different locations. These can pick up the signal, amplify it and spread it out again for more people to receive. It is very much the same when we are dealing with laying on of hands. There are people who will not receive the Holy Spirit until hands are laid on because their faith is not developed or something else is stopping them from receiving the power of God. When hands are laid on, the signal is amplified and the power of the Holy Spirit flows into them.

You are like the switch that turns on the lights. The power is behind the switch, but the switch has to be turned on in order for the lights to come on. When you are there and you are standing between God and the individual as a point of contact, you are the switch. The power flows, and the individual receives.

The power of the Holy Spirit is transmitted through this point of contact in healing as well. Let's look at another situation found in Acts 9 concerning Paul and how he received the Holy Spirit. Saul was persecuting the church until Jesus appeared to him and dealt with him. "And Saul arose from the earth; and when his eyes were opened, he saw no man: but they led him by the hand, and brought him into Damascus" (v. 8).

Saul went from being perhaps the proudest man in the world to being the most humble man in the world. Here was someone who had it all, and suddenly he was lying on the ground, blind. He was the kind of person who always relied on himself for whatever he needed. Then other people had to lead him.

Verse 17 says, "And Ananias went his way, and entered into the house." This is the house that Saul was in. Saul had come into Damascus. God commanded Ananias to seek Saul out and minister to him.

If you read the previous scriptures you find that Ananias was not exactly thrilled with God's request. After all, Saul was a persecutor of the church. Ananias knew he had come to Damascus to imprison Christians and take them back to Jerusalem for trial.

Ananias was obedient to the Lord and went his way. He entered into the house and put his hands on Saul. Believers laid hands on other people because they saw Jesus do the same thing. They followed that tradition after Jesus had returned to the Father. When Ananias saw Saul, he put his hands on him and said, "Brother Saul, the Lord, even Jesus, that appeared unto thee in the way as thou camest, hath sent me, that thou mightest receive thy sight, and be filled with the Holy Ghost. And immediately there fell from his eyes as it had been scales: and he received sight forthwith, and arose, and was baptized" (vv. 17-18).

Two things happened with the laying on of hands. First, Saul received his sight. A gift of healing was operating. Where he had been blind, instantly he received his sight. Second, he was baptized in the Holy Spirit.

Notice that Ananias did not pray a long prayer. He just went to Saul, laid hands on him and said, "Brother Saul, receive your sight, and be filled with the Holy Ghost."

That must have been exciting for a man who just a short while before was persecuting everyone who had anything to do with Christianity. Saul became one of them.

Let's look at Acts 19:1-3. "And it came to pass, that while Apollos was at Corinth, Paul having passed through the upper coasts came to Ephesus: and finding certain disciples, he said unto them, Have ye received the Holy Ghost since ye believed? And they said unto him, We have not so much as heard whether there be any Holy Ghost. And he said unto them, Unto what then were ye baptized? And they said, Unto John's baptism."

John's baptism was a baptism for the repentance of sin, not a believer's baptism in the sense that we baptize believers today. A believer's baptism is a statement of identification with Jesus Christ. The old man is dead, and the new man is raised to new life.

"Then said Paul, John verily baptized with the baptism of repentance, saying unto the people, that they should believe on him which should come after him, that is, on Christ Jesus. When they heard this, they were baptized in the name of the Lord Jesus" (vv. 4-5). They were baptized again. This was the believer's baptism.

"And when Paul had laid his hands upon them, the Holy Ghost came on them; and they spake with tongues, and prophesied" (v. 6). When did this happen? When Paul laid his hands upon them. It does not say Paul led them in a specific prayer to receive the baptism of the Holy Spirit. It says when Paul laid his hands upon them, the Holy Ghost came on them.

The believing Jews were already acquainted with the trinity and the moving of the Holy Spirit. The individuals who had no access to the Hebrew religion and their Scriptures did not know there was any such thing as the Holy Spirit.

The Corinthians only had experience with Jesus and knew about repentance from sin. They had never experienced the Holy Spirit's power. Then they spoke in tongues and prophesied.

With regard to laying on of hands, we also find that not only the transmission of the Holy Spirit occurs, but also healing, as Saul experienced when Ananias prayed.

Jesus healed people in the same way. We find Him laying hands on people throughout the Gospels.

Jesus was extremely interested in being with people and touching them. However, we do not find Him very often laying hands on Pharisees and Sadducees. Not only did they not want to receive what He had, He did not want to receive what they had. But He was quick to lay His hands on individuals who were open to receive from Him and to whom He could transmit the power of the Spirit.

We must learn something about the laying on of hands. Many individuals need healing for their bodies or for victory over a habit. Or perhaps they are having financial trouble. Many times you can lay hands on them and pray all you want and nothing ever changes. Sooner or later you get to the root and find out why they are not helped. More often than not they are cursed because they are not obedient in an area the Bible has spoken about specifically.

Malachi 3 says to "bring all the tithe into the storehouse." If you fail to do so, you are dealt a curse. To many people that sounds harsh. "You mean if I don't bring my money, God isn't going to heal me?" Yes, that is exactly what I mean. You have to do what God says. It is not that God withholds healing but that the devil is there and keeps sickness on your body. Until that curse is broken and people obey God's Word, they are not able to receive. The Bible says very plainly that those who do not tithe and do not give God His portion have a curse on them.

On the other hand, the Bible promises that if you tithe, God will open up the windows of heaven and pour out a blessing that there is not room enough to receive. The devourer will be rebuked.

Sons of God Are Led by the Spirit of God

Once when a lady was in line for prayer for her finances, I asked whether she tithed. "No," she said. "But I'm not a member of this church." I told her, "You don't have to be a member of this church to tithe. You can take your tithe to some other church. We don't want your money, but we want you to be set free. You cannot be set free from this attack of a poverty spirit unless you are willing to walk in accordance with God's Word."

A curse comes when people are not obedient to God's Word. Look at Galatians 3. Not only is the curse mentioned here, but the way of victory as well.

Galatians 3:8-10: "And the scripture, foreseeing that God would justify the heathen through faith, preached before the gospel unto Abraham, saying, In thee shall all nations be blessed. So then they which be of faith are blessed with faithful Abraham. For as many as are of the works of the law are under the curse: for it is written, Cursed is every one that continueth not in all things which are written in the book of the law to do them."

Let's understand one thing about this. Many people say, "We're not under the law anymore; we're under grace." That is true, but the grace of God makes these two statements. If you love God with all your heart, all your soul, all your mind and all your strength and if you love your neighbor as yourself, you will automatically fulfill all the law of the prophets. Jesus never said, "I have come to abolish the law." He said He came to fulfill the law and that the law, the Word of God, would stand forever. Many people reason, "I'm not going to tithe because we're not under the law anymore." And, of course, they found that tithing was instituted before the law.

The Bible says plainly that they are cursed. It is true that we do not live our lives by "thou-shalt-nots." We live by the "do's," which are to love God with all our heart, all our soul, all our mind and all our strength, and to love our neighbors as ourselves. When we do these two things we will not have a problem with the thou-shalt-nots.

The Bible tells us to bring the tithes into the storehouse. If we do so, God will open up the blessings of heaven. If we do not, we will be cursed, and the devourer (Satan) will come. If people want to receive from God but are not tithing, they will not receive until they do.

Some individuals are ignorant of what the Word says about tithing. Ignorance is different from blatant rebellion. Rebellion is a spirit of witchcraft and idolatry. Those people who are in rebellion are not going to receive from God. People who are willing to be educated about the Word and begin to walk and tithe in accordance with God's Word are going to receive.

There is no way to escape the curse of the law if the law is not being fulfilled. The law is fulfilled if we live our lives as we are supposed to by loving God and loving our neighbors. Then we will receive all the benefits. However, if we are deliberately disobedient to God's law, we open up the way for the devourer to come. First John 1:7 says, "But if we walk in the light, as he is in the light, we have fellowship one with another, and the blood of Jesus Christ his Son cleanseth us from all sin."

Individuals who desire to receive need to be tithers. When you are praying for people, be sensitive in this area. It is surprising the number of individuals who do not realize this and how excited people get about it. If we are disobedient to the law, we bring a curse upon ourselves. If we live in accordance with God's Word, we will automatically fulfill the law and not come under the power of that curse.

Consider what Jesus did with regard to laying on of hands when He was ministering to the sick. Matthew 8:14-15 says, "And when Jesus was come into Peter's house, he saw his wife's mother laid, and sick of a fever. And he touched her hand, and the fever left her: and she arose, and ministered unto them."

Note that He touched her hand. He came into contact with her. When He did so, the healing power of God was transmitted to her body. The power of God is first received internally in our spirit; then it is transmitted from us.

We see the reversal of this happening with the woman who had the hemorrhage for twelve years. She said, "If I can touch His garment, if I can just touch the hem of His garment, I will be whole." She reached out with the touch of faith and pulled the power of God into action. Jesus perceived that virtue had gone out of Him, and she was healed instantly.

Jesus did not hold healing services. He walked up, touched people and they were set free from sickness. Laying on of hands was an integral part of His ministry.

In Matthew 9:18 Jesus was speaking about the new covenant. He discussed baptism of the Holy Spirit and a few other things. "While he yet spake these things unto them, behold, there came a certain ruler, and worshipped him, saying, My daughter is even now dead: but come and lay thy hand upon her, and she shall live."

When the word *ruler* is used it indicates an official of the synagogue, someone in authority over the Jews. He said, "If you come and lay Your hand upon my daughter, she'll be made well."

He was aware of transference. We have discussed already how the priest laid his hand on the sacrifice, for instance, to transmit sin. Then he slew the sacrifice. When Jesus was taken in the Garden of Gethsemane, the sinners laid their hands upon Him and transmitted to Him the sin of the world which He bore on the cross.

Jairus came to Jesus and said, "If you'll lay Your hand upon her, she will live." He was aware the life and power of God were present in Jesus.

Physical contact is very important. It is a representation of what God does for us. God actually lives in us. We are in Him. We do not know all the things about it, but we are in constant fellowship with Him. When we touch one another, shake hands, hug or greet one another with a holy kiss as the Bible says, some people take it out of context. But God would not say to do these things if they were not good. However, there are some people we do not want to lay our hands on and, in so doing, participate in their sin.

"And Jesus arose, and followed him, and so did his disciples. And, behold, a woman, which was diseased with an issue of blood twelve years, came behind him, and touched the hem of his garment: For she said within herself, If I may but touch his garment, I shall be whole. But Jesus turned him about, and when he saw her, he said, Daughter, be of good comfort; thy faith hath made thee whole. And the woman was made whole from that hour. And when Jesus came into the ruler's house, and saw the minstrels and the people making a noise, He said unto them, Give place: for the maid is not dead, but sleepeth. And they laughed him to scorn" (vv. 19-24).

They were convinced she was dead. When Jesus said, "She's not dead, but only sleeping," they thought He was crazy.

"But when the people were put forth, he went in, and took her by the hand, and the maid arose" (v. 25). Note that He took her by the hand. Physical contact was made, and she arose.

In Matthew 5, let's look at another area where Jesus dealt with

164

hands. "And if thy right eye offend thee, pluck it out, and cast it from thee: for it is profitable for thee that one of thy members should perish, and not that thy whole body be cast into hell. And if thy right hand offend thee, cut it off, and cast it from thee: for it is profitable for thee that one of thy members should perish, and not that thy whole body should be cast into hell" (vv. 29-30).

Mark 6:1-2 says, "And he went out from thence, and came into his own country; and his disciples follow him. And when the sabbath day was come, he began to teach in the synagogue: and many hearing him were astonished, saying, From whence hath this man these things? and what wisdom is this which is given unto him, that even such mighty works are wrought by his hands?" In the laying on of hands, we allow ourselves to be vessels through which God can touch other people, thereby transmitting His power.

"Is not this the carpenter..." (v. 3). Look at verse 5. "And he could there do no mighty work, save that he laid his hands upon a few sick folk, and healed them."

In Mark 10 people brought children to Jesus. The Spirit that was on Him was imparted to the children. It is important to know what kind of people teach and instruct your children and who touches them, because transference of spirits occurs through touch. However, we should not live in fear. If we are doing our job as parents and keeping the umbrella of protection over our children, spirits will never cause a problem. We should do our best always to put ourselves and our children in a positive environment so that the touch they receive from individuals will be positive and encouraging.

Parents were specifically interested in having Jesus touch the children because they knew the children would benefit if Jesus came into contact with them. His spirit was transferred upon them.

"...And his disciples rebuked those that brought them. But when Jesus saw it, he was much displeased, and said unto them, Suffer the little children to come unto me, and forbid them not: for of such is the kingdom of God. Verily I say unto you, Whosoever shall not receive the kingdom of God as a little child, he shall not enter therein. And he took them up in his arms, put his hands upon them, and blessed them" (Mark 10:13-16). He put His hands upon them and blessed them. He did it deliberately. A blessing was transferred upon them. Surely those children He touched obtained success later in life.

In Mark 16 we find an awareness of the power of God. Mark 16:17-18 says, "And these signs shall follow them that believe; in my name shall they cast out devils; they shall speak with new tongues; they shall take up serpents; and if they drink any deadly thing, it shall not hurt them; they shall lay hands on the sick, and they shall recover."

This is our command from Jesus Himself, to lay hands on the sick that they might recover.

In Acts 14, a transference of God's power through the laying on of hands occurs. "And it came to pass in Iconium, that they went both together into the synagogue of the Jews, and so spake, that a great multitude both of the Jews and also of the Greeks believed. But the unbelieving Jews stirred up the Gentiles, and made their minds evil affected [or opposed] against the brethren. Long time therefore abode they speaking boldly in the Lord, which gave testimony unto the word of his grace, and granted signs and wonders to be done by their hands" (vv. 1-3).

Signs and wonders are a testimony to the Word of God. Read through to the end of Mark 16 and you will find that Jesus confirmed His Word with signs and wonders. These signs and wonders were done by the hands of those individuals who preached the Word.

Many times when we lay hands on people, signs and wonders occur. When a tumor disappears, that is a sign and a wonder. When people have their teeth filled supernaturally by the power of God, that is a sign and a wonder.

God's Thoughts Will Be Your Thoughts

When we lay hands on people we impart God's power. It is important that we stay charged up in the Word of God by studying the Word and also praying in other tongues. That way, when we lay our hands on people, there is something to give out. If we lay hands on people and have nothing to give out, we open ourselves for an attack, for something to come in. On the other hand, if we are overflowing with the Spirit and His power, the laying on of our hands will transmit that power.

With a few minor modifications, a radio transmitter can be turned into a receiver, and vice versa. The same applies to us as believers. We can either transmit the power of God or we can receive other false powers. When you are laying hands on people, your spirit is very open and you can receive if you do not have something going out. Stay filled up with the Word and the Holy Spirit, and that risk will not bother you. You will stay free and not have other spirits transferred upon you.

Acts 19:11 says, "And God wrought special miracles by the hands of Paul." The word *special* means "unusual." All miracles are unusual to me. God did something tremendous. A miracle is something that cannot be explained by natural law. God did this through Paul's hands. Whenever Paul laid hands on people, they were set free.

In the next verse we find that even cloths, aprons and handkerchiefs were taken from his body to the bodies of those who were sick, and they were healed by the power of God that flowed out from the cloths. The power of God is transferable, and the Spirit of God is transferable.

It is scriptural for a minister under the anointing of God to take a cloth, pray over it and lay his hands on it, because the anointing of God is transferable.

Just because someone sends you a square of cloth does not mean there is any anointing in it. I am not commenting on anyone who

167

does it or does not do it. I have done this in the past. I have had requests for this. If someone writes and wants us to send them a cloth, we will pray over it and send it out.

Wholesale distribution of pieces of fabric makes you a fabric store and not a minister. If all you are going to do is send out pieces of cloth, it is like distributing kosher food. It is prepared in a certain way, but what makes it kosher is that the rabbi comes and blesses the whole warehouse. The warehouse gets blessed, and the food gets blessed, but it is not done individually. He does not lay his hand on every pickle that comes out. But prayer cloths are certainly viable. However, I have my doubts about holy water from the well of Bethlehem and other gimmicky things that people use.

Personal ministry is much better than cloths. Church service is much better than television. As wonderful as television is, we cannot preach the gospel in the way the gospel needs to be preached around the world just on television.

In some healing services, people sitting in the congregation are healed. God does not have to do things a certain way. He will perform His miracles whatever way He wants to. Notice, too, that most people who come for healing are unbelievers, not knowing the Lord, and they are healed in some miraculous way. Signs and wonders are a testimony to unbelievers, not believers. Believers certainly should not need it. The Pharisees and Sadducees were always coming to Jesus, saying, "Give us a sign."

Mark 6:13 speaks about anointing with oil. Does the application of oil with the hand have something to do with the healing? When you anoint with oil, you have to use your hand. Is the anointing coming through the hands or the oil?

First of all, people in the Old Testament did not anoint the way we anoint, and possibly not so in the New Testament. Anointing in the Old Testament was done by pouring a flask of oil over the top of the head. When we anoint with oil, the oil represents the Holy Spirit, just as baptism in water represents Jesus' death, burial and

168

resurrection. It also represents death to the old self and being raised to new life. The oil represents the Holy Spirit. We anoint with oil, but not all the time. It depends on the situation.

The Bible says in James that if someone is sick, let him call for the elders of the church, that he might be anointed with oil and prayed over. The oil, representative of the Holy Spirit, is a point of contact, just as a cloth might be.

CHAPTER TWELVE

We Live in Two Worlds

Some people brush aside the subject of spirits as if it were unimportant, nonexistent or some sort of abnormal mental exercise. Before you negate the reality and importance of the spiritual world, consider several factors. The only one who would not want you to know the truth about the spirit world is the devil. He wants to keep you blind to its reality while he does his dirty work.

When you are aware of spiritual things, you are aware of the Spirit of God and the spirit of the devil. You are able to recognize these spirits and deal with them. You are able to stand against them, and you are not afraid or confused. The devil would have us afraid and confused.

We live in two worlds, the physical world and the spiritual world. The physical world is easily understood because it is clearly evident all around us.

While we cannot generally see or hear spirits with our natural eyes and ears, we can sometimes perceive them. The natural eye sees natural things, and natural ears hear natural things. Spirits manifest themselves on occasion, making it possible for us to see and hear them. I have been in meetings where I could see angels all around the room. Nobody else could see them. The spirit has senses. We can even smell the Holy Spirit. It has a sweet fragrance. There are times when the Spirit of God moves by me and I can smell His fragrance. I know He is there. I can talk to Him. I have had Him sit in my car. I could not see Him with my natural eyes, but I knew He was there. I could feel His presence.

Physical World Is for the Natural Man

Because God is a Spirit, we have to acknowledge and believe that there is a spiritual realm in which God dwells. Jesus, also being a Spirit, took on flesh so that He could teach us how to relate to the spirit realm and so that He could relate to the physical realm.

God had to put on flesh to know just how severe the attacks of the enemy are and how much man can endure. In order for God to understand our feelings, He had to become as we are. When we cry out to Him, He knows exactly what is happening to us. God sent His only Son so that He could understand humanity and we would have an intercessor, a mediator, to intercede on our behalf. An angel cannot be our mediator or intercessor because an angel could never understand our feelings and our challenges, but Jesus can because he was not only one of us but he suffered, died and rose again from the dead for us (See Hebrews 4:14-16).

First Corinthians 2:11-12 tells us there are three different spirits: the Spirit of God, the spirit of man (Balaam, which is the soul) and the spirit of the world. The devil can only get to you through the flesh. Why? Because the flesh is the only part that has not been redeemed.

Your mind, your will and your intellect can be renewed by the Word. Your spirit has been saved. That is the area where you and I are created in the image of God. When God interjects His Spirit by our invitation, He comes in and our spirit is immediately transformed. It is an infant stage.

You need to nourish and protect the infant spirit just as you would a child. The spirit can be bruised, wounded and hurt. It is real. But if you have been born again, it is the one part of you that the devil cannot touch. However, he never stops attacking, depriving, harassing and tormenting you. Why? He wants you to go back to where you were before. The devil can only attack you when you allow him to do so through ignorance or choice. Ephesians 4:27 says, "Neither give place to the devil."

The flesh has chemical compositions in it just as the earth does. You will find at least sixteen different elements in the flesh that are also in the earth. We can prove by this that man was created out of the dust of the earth. The devil knows the weak areas in your life. Why? Because the flesh has not been redeemed. The flesh, as it is right now, will not go to heaven. It will have to die first and be resurrected by God. We will then be glorified and see Him as He is. Until then we have to learn to cope with our flesh.

First John 5:18 says, "We know that whosoever is born of God sinneth not; but he that is begotten of God keepeth himself, and that wicked one touched him not." This is a scripture that every Christian should memorize. When you are born of God, the devil cannot touch you. Why, then, do we experience so much difficulty? Why is there so much temptation in the world? God did not say the devil cannot tempt you. That is one thing he has a legal right to do.

In Slavic languages there is a word that is more meaningful to me than its counterpart in English. The word is *zackalyonij*. *Zackalyonij* means "hardened or tempered steel." Such steel is so tough that nothing can bend it. Christians have to be hardened. The devil will try to see whether or not you are really hardened in the Word.

173

You cannot stop the devil from tempting or deceiving you. But you can make him miserable by countering him with the Word. He'll leave you for a season when you put the Word on him. If you do not have the Word, if you are not *zackalyonij,* he will test you to see just how long you can keep your edge on. If your edge becomes dull, he will come and torment you. He knows the flesh is weak.

Man has a free will to choose. He can choose the devil or God. No one can force him. He has to make the decision. He can come to church and physically sit in church but not be in church spiritually. His mind may be somewhere playing golf. You can lock a man in prison, but if he is free spiritually, the prison will not bother him because he is free.

The devil knows that man's flesh needs to be admired, appreciated and stroked. It would be foolish for any Christian to say that the flesh is not important. We have to have the flesh to live on this earth. At the same time, we must understand there is constant pressure and temptation on the flesh. Often those pressures come in such a subtle way that we do not even think they are wrong. The devil doesn't walk up and say, "Here I am with horns, pitchfork and tail wearing a red suit, and I'm going to tempt you to commit adultery." He is smarter than that. He will say, "Oh, but you're so important in the body of Christ. Look how God uses you. You lay hands on people, and zap, they just go down. You should take the position of the pastor." He will put you on a pedestal and tell you how important you are. If he gets you thinking in any of these areas, he has you listening to him, which is what he wants. If you are not mature in the Lord, you will listen and agree with the devil. Once you agree, BANG!—he has an entry into you, and he will feed you all kinds of garbage.

The only One who gives us recognition and position is God! When men recognize your ability and ask you to take a position, it is a different story. Then you are not blowing your own trumpet. Someone else is.

All Christians want to be used of God. All Christians go through periods of growth, then all of a sudden it seems as if everything comes to a standstill. They pray and nothing happens. Nothing changes. They say, "Has God forgotten me? What am I doing wrong?" What we must realize is this: When you were an infant, someone else had to feed you and clean your dirty diapers. Someone else had to take care of you and provide for you. But now that you have grown some, you should be able to feed and dress yourself. When you were ten weeks old, someone else had to do everything for you. When you were ten years old, you did some of these things yourself.

Let's take this from the natural to the supernatural. When you are born again, you know you are going to heaven. Things become new in your life. The Father provides everything. He changes your diapers. He wipes your nose. He is there all the time. Once you start growing in the Lord, He lets you try your wings, so to speak. You will feel awkward, but He is always there. He is allowing you to realize you can do some things on your own. You can put on your shoes now. You can feed yourself. When you reach a plateau area, God is simply allowing you to take your own steps. The devil knows that, and he will come at that moment and say, "Nobody cares! Nobody loves you! Nobody recognizes you! They don't recognize your gifts. They don't give you a position. They don't ask you to do anything, and they certainly are not grateful for what you are doing!" When the devil attacks this way, you must have enough of the Word in you to discern what is happening.

John 1 shows us that Jesus took on physical flesh so that He could relate to the needs of the physical being.

"In the beginning was the Word, and the Word was with God, and the Word was God. The same was in the beginning with God. All things were made by him; and without him was not any thing made that was made. In him was life; and the life was the light of men" (vv. 1-4).

Verse 14 of the same chapter says, "And the Word was made

flesh, and dwelt among us, (and we beheld his glory, the glory as of the only begotten of the Father,) full of grace and truth."

John 1 verifies that the Spirit took on flesh. If the Spirit came before the flesh, it is obvious that the Spirit is more knowledgeable and more powerful than the flesh. Therefore, the flesh can be, and is, influenced by the Spirit. If you put information into a computer, the computer stores the information. By pushing certain buttons the information can be retrieved. It will produce exactly what was put into it. Your flesh reacts according to what is in it. It is going to obey. Whatever you put in is going to come out. Whatever starts manifesting in the flesh was put there beforehand by you or someone else. Even if someone else put it in, you allowed them to do it. You are in control. You cannot blame anyone else.

In Revelation 19:1-2 John says, "And after these things I heard a great voice of much people in heaven, saying, Alleluia; Salvation, and glory, and honour, and power, unto the Lord our God: For true and righteous are his judgments." Verse 13 says, "And he was clothed with a vesture dipped in blood: and his name is called The Word of God." When I say know the Word, what I mean is know Jesus. When I say know Jesus, I am saying to know the Word. They are one and the same.

The Spirit was there before the flesh came into existence. Isaiah 9:6 says, "For unto us a child is born,..." Remember Isaiah was prophesying in the Old Testament. He was saying something that had not yet happened. He was foretelling something that would happen in the future. However, in the spirit it had already happened. Isaiah was including himself and the Israelites. "For unto us...," he said. He didn't say, "For unto them in the future."

Follow this thought. Isaiah says, "...a child is born..." That is present tense. Was Isaiah telling the truth or lying? In the natural realm, you would ask how a child could be born to the Israelites when Jesus was not yet born. Yet he said, "For unto us a child is born..." Then he goes on to say, "...unto us a son is given." The Son was given, but a child was born. Those are two different things. This means that people before the New Testament had the privilege of knowing Jesus Christ as their Lord, as their Prince of Peace, even as we do today. The difference is that then He was only in the Spirit, because the Son was already given. Every time you see the Angel of the Lord appear in Scripture, it refers to Jesus Christ Himself. The pillar of fire was Christ. The burning bush was Christ. He was appearing to them in a Spirit form.

Philippians 2:6-7 says, "Who, being in the form of God, thought it not robbery to be equal with God: But made himself of no reputation, and took upon him the form of a servant, and was made in the likeness of men." Even though He put on flesh and became as we are, it was not wrong for Him to be God. He was still God, yet He was just as much a human being as you or me.

We see, then, that Jesus Christ came into the earth as a human being but still had the power of the Spirit within Him. He was limited to what He could do and where He could be in the physical realm, but He was not limited in the spirit realm. Neither are we limited in the spirit realm.

Spiritual World Is for the Spiritual Man

Your spirit is not bound unless you bind it. If you release your spirit, your spirit can pray for your loved ones and the saints around the world. It is not limited. It is only limited by your will.

It is described very clearly how Jesus came into being and how He put on flesh. Matthew 1:18 says, "Now the birth of Jesus Christ was on this wise: When as his mother Mary was espoused to Joseph, before they came together, she was found with child of the Holy Ghost." Before they had a husband-wife relationship, she was found with child. She was pregnant of the Holy Spirit. "Then Joseph her husband, being a just man, and not willing to make her a public example, was minded to put her away privily" (v. 19).

Joseph was very thoughtful and very concerned. He was also very selfish. He was just another man. He was trying to protect himself, not Mary. How would Joseph explain to everybody that Mary was pregnant? The law stated that if a person committed adultery or fornication, he or she would be stoned to death. Joseph was not stupid. He did not want to die. He thought if he could take Mary away without telling anyone, he could stay alive. The Holy Spirit did not tell him to do that. Joseph decided for himself. Joseph was going to take care of this embarrassing situation privately. But God knows all things.

"But while he thought on these things, behold, an angel of the Lord appeared unto him in a dream, saying, Joseph, thou son of David, fear not to take unto thee Mary thy wife; for that which is conceived in her is of the Holy Ghost. And she shall bring forth a son, and thou shalt call his name Jesus: for he shall save his people from their sins" (vv. 20-21).

All the books of the Old Testament had prophesied about Jesus. Then He came to dwell in the flesh. But before He became flesh He was a Spirit.

First Timothy 3:16 says, "And without controversy great is the mystery of godliness: God was manifest in the flesh, justified in the Spirit, seen of angels, preached unto the Gentiles, believed on in the world, received up into glory."

How may a person love God and do things for the Lord then turn around and do just the opposite? How may a person serve the Lord and preach the gospel, then all of a sudden turn completely around? We know how powerful the flesh is. The devil cannot come into you unless you allow him to do so. He comes through deception, position, wealth, riches and other temptations. He has a legal right to tempt you. But you have the legal right to keep him out. When we learn how to keep him out, we will be much more effective for the kingdom of God.

CHAPTER THIRTEEN

Laying on of Hands can Be A Blessing or a Curse

There are specific reasons why we lay hands on people. In this chapter we will study the laying on of hands as it relates to the transference of spirits. Laying on of hands was used among the Jews under the old covenant and by the early believers under the new covenant.

Have you ever considered what life would be like if you had no hands? Think of all the things you would not be able to do. The Bible speaks many times about the hand of God. For example, David said, "Thy right hand and thy holy arm have given me the victory." Hands play a prominent role in the Scriptures. Over fifteen hundred separate references to hands can be found in both the Old and New Testaments.

Following is a list of Scripture references where hands are mentioned:

1. Leading hands: Acts 9:8

2. Killing hands: Numbers 11:15. Moses was speaking to the people who had a problem with him. He was pointing out that there are killing hands—people who use their hands to bring on destruction to the flesh, actually murdering hands.
3. Working hands: Ezra 5:8; Genesis 31:42
4. Innocent hands: Genesis 20:5
5. Offering hands: Numbers 5:18
6. Clapping hands: 2 Kings 11:12
7. Clean hands: Job 9:30; Psalm 24:4
8. Stretched-out hands: Psalm 44:20
9. Betraying hands: Luke 22:21
10. Hands of sinful men: Luke 24:7
11. Cursed hands: Matthew 25:41

The following do not have specific Scripture references listed:

13. Loving hands
14. Gentle hands
15. Holding hands
16. Smooth hands
17. Praying hands
18. Powerful hands
19. Blessing hands
20. Serving hands
21. Wicked hands

You might want to study each type in the Scripture with the help of a concordance.

When we talk about laying on of hands, there are both blessings and dangers involved. Many individuals, especially when they first find out about laying on of hands, want to lay hands on everybody. They want to be a blessing. They want to get involved in ministry. This is good, but we must realize there are dangers just as there are blessings. Laying on of hands involves transference of supernatural power. We are transferring either a positive force or a negative force. It is also possible that a particular spirit may try to transfer to you.

Laying on of hands is a basic Bible doctrine. It is one of the doctrines Paul spoke about in Hebrews 6:1-2: "Therefore leaving the principles of the doctrine of Christ, let us go on unto perfection; not laying again the foundation of repentance from dead works, and of faith toward God. Of the doctrine of baptisms, and of laying on of hands, and of resurrection of the dead, and of eternal judgment."

Paul was exhorting the Hebrews not just to continue with the basics but to move on to other things. He gives a specific description of the basic doctrines of the church. We know the foundation of repentance from dead works and faith toward God are basic doctrines of the church.

Paul puts the laying on of hands along with faith and resurrection of the dead, baptism in water, baptism in the Holy Spirit and all the basic things we need to do. If it is grouped together with faith, salvation and resurrection of the dead, it must be very important. If it is very important, we must learn how it works and how we can use it effectively in ministry.

When we lay our hands on someone, there are several possibilities:
1. We can impart to them a good spirit or impart to them the power of God.
2. We can impart to them a negative spirit.
3. We can receive from their spirit.

Let's look specifically at the negative transference of spirits. Consider the following scenarios, and see if you recognize any of them. These are all real-life situations.

A minister is having difficulty with immorality in his own life (adultery, fornication and lust) but ministers to other people in those same situations. Couples who come to be counseled by him find he has imparted those same spirits to them. Their situations, instead of getting better, become worse. They probably leave consultation more confused than when they came. Because the minister has not cleansed his own life of that particular sin, the door is open for the transference of that spirit even, in some cases, where it was not a problem in the beginning.

I am not saying that someone else can manipulate you. You still must make your own choices. But that spirit can be transferred.

Let's consider another situation. The leader of a prayer group develops a critical spirit. Suddenly all the members of the prayer group begin to develop the same critical spirit. They also get an unholy affection for the leader, cleave to that leader and join together in a critical spirit.

Galatians 5:14-15 says, "For all the law is fulfilled in one word, even in this; Thou shalt love thy neighbour as thyself. But if ye bite and devour one another, take heed that ye be not consumed one of another."

None of us would go out and have human flesh for lunch. We know this is not what the Scripture is saying. It is talking about spiritual cannibalism. When we enter into a critical spirit, that spirit can be transferred to people who fellowship with us and who respond to our leadership. They begin to bite and devour. Then everyone is consumed by the same spirit. In the scenario of the prayer group, the negative spirit was transferred from the leader upon others, and they began to speak negatively about one another. That devouring spirit was loosed, and they consumed one another in a passion to defame and destroy.

When we are involved in the laying on of hands, it is extremely important that we realize the kind of spirit we are imparting to other individuals as well. If we are not pure when we lay hands on people, we take the risk of transmitting not only the power of God but also a negative spirit or even a poor attitude that might exist within us.

Let's consider another scenario. A homosexual evangelist lays hands on people, and some of those individuals begin to have homosexual tendencies. That spirit was transferred to the people by the homosexual evangelist.

Another situation: A layman who has gone astray in doctrine decides he wants to develop his own way. He leads others astray, and a cult group emerges.

The individual who founded Jehovah's Witnesses started off as a basic Christian believer, then became a Seventh-Day Adventist and later a Jehovah's Witness. He developed his own doctrine and drew people away with him.

A layman can start to feel he has knowledge. After all, it's the same Word. God regards us all the same. He may say, "I don't need training because the Bible says let no one despise your youth," or "I have no need of anyone to teach me because I have the Holy Spirit," etc. Such a person may draw others to him, and his spirit is imparted to them. He ministers to them by laying his hands on them. Through that point of contact, a spirit of erroneous doctrine is transmitted to the people.

Let's consider another situation. A high-strung, emotionally imbalanced woman ministers to women, and soon the spirit of the one ministering is imparted to those to whom she ministers. Something such as this could occur in a home prayer group when a person feels he (or she) has a call from God. He starts a Bible study, but since he is wound up tighter than an eight-day clock, there is no peace. There is no love. There is no joy. Individuals who have this kind of agitated spirit will transfer that same spirit to the individuals to whom they minister.

God was able to transfer the spirit that was upon Moses onto those he had selected to minister. That transference took place because that is the way God works. God takes a leader and He multiplies him. His desire is to multiply the ministry of that leader through other people working in conjunction with him so that the work of the gospel can be done. It is impossible for one person to do it all. The call of God on your life might be so powerful and so big it would be impossible for you to do it alone. You have to get other people involved so they will help you fulfill that call.

First Timothy 5:22 says, "Lay hands suddenly on no man, neither be partaker of other men's sins: keep thyself pure."

We lay hands on people for many different reasons. We lay hands on the sick so they will recover. We lay hands on people to send them into their ministry and to set them apart for the Lord. We lay hands on people to receive them into membership of the church.

You should not be quick to lay hands on someone for the sake of ministry. You might end up being a partaker of their sins, the Bible says. "Lay hands suddenly on no man." There are individuals, for instance, who get upset because we do not ordain them in the ministry. Perhaps they have been waiting for two or three years, but we still do not have God's consent to lay hands on them and set them apart in ministry. When we do that we become a partaker of their ministry. If you are a person in authority, never jump at the chance to lay hands on someone to send them into ministry. The instant you do that, you indicate your approval of that person's ministry, and you may also open yourself up to the spirit that permeates him as well. If you are not comfortable with an individual's spirit, you should never lay hands on him. You should not lay hands on people until you are comfortable with the spirit that is in them. You do not want to be a partaker of their sins.

Suppose we lay hands on an individual, thereby putting our stamp of approval upon him, and he goes off and does things contrary to Scripture. That, of course, is going to reflect upon us. So do not rush out and lay hands on just anybody.

There have been times when people have come up in the healing line and I did not want to touch them with a twenty-foot pole because of the spirit within them. On one such occasion, I told an individual to go sit down and I would minister to him last. His spirit was such that, had I attempted to minister to him then, it would have spoiled the rest of the service, and other people would not have been ministered to. That particular spirit would have attracted a lot of attention to itself and diverted the people's attention from what God was doing. There was no way I was going to put my hands on that person and minister to him until last. That does not mean he did not have needs. If you are ministering to people and they can't tell you what they want from God, they will not receive anything. Satan may even place people in the midst of your ministry to try to throw it off base.

As you go down a healing line, be sensitive about whom you lay your hands on and whom you do not. If you are charged up with the Word of God and the Word is strong in you, you can lay hands on people without fear. On the other hand, many ministers make the mistake of ministering hour after hour under the anointing, until they become weak mentally and physically. Then they come up to someone at the end of the line who has a strong spirit. It can really affect them.

I've heard of ministers who committed suicide after lengthy ministering under the anointing. A spirit came upon them and brought on depression so deep they felt they had no reason to live anymore. These events are rare, but they do happen.

When you are ministering to people under the anointing of God, you are very open, and you must protect yourself. This is one of the reasons we have ushers who are bodyguards. You may be ministering to someone, and someone else may be sneaking up behind you with a knife. There are demon spirits that desire to destroy those who minister under the anointing and look for that opportunity. You must always be aware that this ministry is a real battle. Be sensitive to the Spirit of God, and let God lead you in each particular situation. If you are not wise, you will find your ministry hampered.

You may encounter people with certain spirits and find you can almost discern their thought patterns. The Spirit of God moves, and you become aware of what is happening with them spiritually. When you are open in the Spirit and perceiving things

185

supernaturally, you may receive the thoughts of others. If you are not charged up in the Word when you minister, sometimes those thoughts can enter in and war against you. It is not a very comfortable thing to have to stop and do battle in your mind when there are one hundred people standing in line waiting for you to minister to their needs.

If you ever have the idea that you are God's anointed one and that everyone you lay hands on is going to fall on the floor, I can guarantee that you will fail.

Vessels of the Holy Spirit

If you approach the laying on of hands with the sense that you are a vessel to be used as a transmitter for God's power, you will succeed. There is nothing in the natural that qualifies you to be a minister of the gospel or to lay hands on people. What qualifies you is that you have been born again, that the Spirit of God is awake in your spirit and your spirit is in touch with God. God can then send His anointing through your spirit, which you can transmit by physical contact to the individual in need.

We know the natural man does not comprehend the things of God at all. If you feel that every time you lay hands on people they are going to be healed instantly, what will you think when that does not happen? What is going to happen when you lay hands on people and their pain doesn't leave? What is going to happen when you lay hands on them and they say, "He must not be anointed"?

If your faith is in God and you approach the laying on of hands with a spirit of prayer and humility, realizing you are only a vessel and not the one who possesses the power, then what people say or do is not going to affect you. You lay hands on people because the Word says to do it and because you know God is going to confirm His Word no matter what the people do. The gift of God does not belong to you but is for other people. The more you approach the laying on of hands that way, the more success you will have. God does not need your help. He needs you to yield to Him so He can flow through you, but He does not need your suggestions of a better way. God has good ideas. When we allow ourselves to be vessels for Him, we are able to minister and see other people set free.

The guidance and direction of the Holy Spirit should be sought at every stage. Suppose you notice someone in a healing line who has a specific problem that will take a lengthy time of ministry. There are other people waiting. They have needs. If you take half an hour to minister to that one person, you will lose the thirty or forty who are waiting. Instead, have that person sit down and minister to him at the end. Let God direct to whom you should minister the laying on of hands.

Some people believe that being slain in the Spirit is not real. I don't even like the word *slain. Falling under the power* is much better. There are those who believe ministers actually push people over and that is why they fall to the floor. They do not believe it is the power of God.

I know ministers who push people. I have been pushed. I ministered with a man who was close to three hundred pounds. He would pray in the Spirit, go up to people, lay his hand on the top of their heads and give them a shove while he said, "Come out in Jesus' name!" He practically threw them onto the floor. There was no way to tell whether it was the Spirit of God or not. It probably was, since most of them were not injured. The point is, we do not need to help God in the anointing by pushing people.

Because of situations like this, many people doubt that falling under the power is real. You might be ministering and hear God say, "Don't lay hands on that individual, but speak the Word of healing to him." He might fall right out under the power, depending upon how the Spirit is moving. Just because our tradition is to lay hands on the sick does not mean we have to lay hands on them all the time. God's power will operate whether you touch someone or not.

God may instruct you whether to lay hands on someone. It may be because of the way He wants to deal with them. It might also be that He does not want you to deal with the problem at that time. You must be sensitive to His leading.

What about when people fall on their own, not from the power of God? How do you recognize that?

Some people have been trained through their Pentecostal background that any time they are ministered to they must fall under the power to receive. Consequently, whenever someone comes near them, they buckle their knees and fall. In the midst of all the excitement, sometimes desiring to appear more spiritual, they fall on the floor before the minister gets to them. People have been injured doing such things. I know a lady who had broken ribs because of this. These individuals determine that they are going to receive no matter what, so they help God along and fall on their own. If you perceive that this is the case, make sure there are people to catch them.

Sometimes the anointing of God moves so powerfully that it knocks you over like a hurricane blast. Other times it is a gentle nudge. Some individuals resist that nudge and remain standing, whereas others yield to it and fall.

Just because one remains standing and another falls does not mean that both have not received. Everybody receives from the Holy Spirit based upon what they are accustomed to. Some people want all of God that they can get. They have a real sweet spirit before God. They will receive from the slightest nudge God gives them and fall under the power. There are others who have never received from the Spirit. They lock their knees, saying, "God isn't going to knock me over," or "If He does, it's really going to be God."

Remember these questions: Who do you pray for? When do you pray for them? How do you pray for them? We are not bound to do things the same way all the time. If you do things the same way all the time you get into a rut. That can become a tradition.

The Healing Touch

The believer who lays on hands must know how to claim on behalf of his own spirit the continual purifying and protecting power of the blood of Christ. We must protect our own spirits from negative spirits when we lay hands on people. This is done by understanding the ministry of Jesus and the cleansing blood of Christ.

The Bible says we are overcomers by the blood of the Lamb and the word of our testimony. Strive to keep yourself pure when you minister to others, and do not allow any unconfessed sin to remain in your life. Do not allow any habit to control you.

First John 1:5 says, "This then is the message which we have heard of him, and declare unto you, that God is light, and in him is no darkness at all."

God is light, and in Him is absolutely no darkness. That is why He can always minister effectively to everybody. He has no sin or difficulty with blind spots. In Him there is no darkness at all.

First John 1:6 says, "If we say that we have fellowship with him, and walk in darkness, we lie, and do not the truth." Notice the phrase *walk in darkness*. Very few of us would go out on a pitch-black night without a light or venture into an unlit cave. We know that if we go into the darkness we might stumble or fall and cause harm to our bodies. As believers we should not walk in darkness. Allowing continual sin to possess us or blind us is walking in darkness. To continue in sin after having received the knowledge that a thing is wrong is to walk in darkness. The Bible does not say you will never pass through darkness or that darkness will never assail you. From time to time you might make a mistake. It's one thing to walk into a dark cave, realize it is dark and come back out. It is quite another to walk straight into the cave to your own destruction.

If we say we have a relationship with God yet continue to walk in bondage to sin, John says that we lie and do not the truth. Verse 7 says, "But if we walk in the light, as he is in the light, we have fellowship one with another, and the blood of Jesus Christ his Son cleanseth us from all sin."

We know that if we abide in Jesus and His words abide in us, we will ask whatever we will and it shall be done for us. If we walk in the light we will not fulfill the lust of the flesh (see Gal. 5:16).

Verse 9 says, "If we confess our sins, he is faithful and just to forgive us our sins, and to cleanse us from all unrighteousness." We confess our mistakes, and God cleanses us and actually purges from us that feeling of unrighteousness.

There are sins we may be committing that we know nothing about simply because we do not have the knowledge necessary to deal with them. The Bible says people perish and go into captivity for lack of knowledge. However, it also says that if we walk in the light as He is in the light, we will have fellowship with our brethren, and the blood of Jesus will cleanse us from all sin.

Sins of commission are the ones you know you are doing. Sins of omission are those you are not aware of. Sometimes we hurt people when we do not intend to hurt them. We know it is not right to hurt people, but sometimes we are not aware that this is happening. When we walk in the light and get close to Jesus, the blood of Jesus cleanses us from all sin, even the things we don't know about. It is extremely dangerous to walk in darkness.

Jesus died not so that He could cover our sin but so that He could forever wash it away and cleanse our knowledge of that sin. Paul wrote in Hebrews that the sacrifices of animals could never take away the remembrance of sin. Sin was always there. It was an ugly stain for all to see. The remembrance of that sin could not be taken away. But Jesus can take away the remembrance of sin. That is why Paul was able to say he had wronged no man even though he had been a murderer. He was able to say that because the blood of Jesus had taken away the very remembrance of that sin.

When we lay on hands, we must be pure and have a good attitude. Do not ever minister to others if you know there is sin in your life that has not been dealt with. It is dangerous for you, and it is dangerous for them. It does not make any difference whether you have a five-fold ministry or whether you are just praying for a friend. Do not allow that sin to dwell in you.

Here is another reason. First John 3:18-22 says, "My little children, let us not love in word, neither in tongue; but in deed and in truth. And hereby we know that we are of the truth, and shall assure our hearts before him. For if our heart condemn us, God is greater than our heart, and knoweth all things. Beloved, if our heart condemn us not, then have we confidence toward God. And whatsoever we ask, we receive of him, because we keep his commandments, and do those things that are pleasing in his sight."

As a believer your spirit is alive unto God. Do you know that your spirit can be grieved if you continually allow the flesh and the mind to overrule it and do things that are ungodly? Your own heart may become grieved and begin to condemn you. Even when your heart condemns you, God is able to set you free from that condemnation. Romans 8:1-2 says, "There is therefore now no condemnation to them which are in Christ Jesus, who walk not after the flesh, but after the Spirit. For the law of the Spirit of life in Christ Jesus hath made me free from the law of sin and death."

First John 3:21 says, "...If our heart condemn us not, then have we confidence toward God." If we stand before God to minister to others and our hearts condemn us not, then we have confidence before God. When you stand in that kind of confidence, the devil won't hang around. The people you minister to will be set free.

The reason why a lot of people never minister effectively is because they do not have that confidence. Something is not right in their relationship with God.

God desires that we walk in confidence before Him. When we

understand what the blood has done for us, we will no longer be in bondage to sin. There is no way for any demon spirit to enter in and affect you when you have been cleansed and sanctified by the blood of the Lamb. But allowing sin to continue in your life robs you of your confidence, and you risk having other spirits imparted to you as well.

A believer who lays hands on others must be so empowered by the Holy Spirit that he is able to overcome any kind of evil spiritual influence seeking to work in or through the one upon whom hands are laid. You must remember the truth of 1 John 4:4: "Greater is he that is in you, than he that is in the world." Luke 10:19 says we have been given authority to "tread on serpents and scorpions, and over all the power of the enemy." Acts 10:38 says, "How God anointed Jesus of Nazareth with the Holy Ghost and with power: who went about doing good, and healing all that were oppressed of the devil."

Let us renew our mind to the consciousness that we have power and authority over the devil so that when we lay hands on people, no matter what spirit they may have, that spirit will recognize our authority in the Word of God and not attempt to transfer to us. It is like wearing armor.

We have faith and confidence that God is going to do what He said He would do. He has said, "Greater is he that is in you, than he that is in the world." He has given you authority to tread on serpents and scorpions and over all the power of the enemy. No demon spirit has the ability to afflict a Christian unless the Christian is unaware of his rights and authority in Jesus Christ.

When you take the time to get the Scriptures into your mind, there is no way a spirit can be transferred to you because you understand your righteousness, your position with God and the authority He has given you. You can then minister successfully to others.

Unless these safeguards are observed, harmful spiritual results may follow the practice of laying on of hands. Unless you are protected and aware of the things we have discussed, there is a very real possibility that instead of blessing other people when you lay hands on them, you may actually do harm to yourself. Or you might transfer to them spiritual influences that you have not dealt with in your own life.

HEREDITARY TRAITS

CHAPTER FOURTEEN

Recognizing Spiritual Influence

There are blessings and dangers involved in the laying on of hands. Paul teaches in 1 Timothy 5 how important this is: "I charge thee before God, and the Lord Jesus Christ, and the elect angels, that thou observe these things without preferring one before another, doing nothing by partiality. Lay hands suddenly on no man, neither be partaker of other men's sins: keep thyself pure" (vv. 21-22).

Paul is telling us not to let others get us under their control. Sometimes, even if it is wrong, a minister will pronounce a blessing on someone because that individual has such a strong power over him. Perhaps the person is providing the minister things in the natural. The person may do that to lure the minister away from God, to drain him of God's power. The devil does not like those who serve God. He will do anything he can to take them away from God.

In other words, if you do not allow yourself to be subjected to the control of others, your spirit and your mind will not be polluted. But if you willingly or even through the lack of knowledge submit yourself or get involved with individuals with a wrong spirit, you will eventually become as they are and a transference of spirit will take place. Proverbs 13:20 says, "He that walketh with wise men shall be wise." The opposite side of that is also true; He that walketh with fools shall be a fool. You might say "I did not know that it should happen to me, or I don't want to be like he is." That is why the Bible tells us to test the spirits, whether they be of God of or the devil.

Hosea 4:6 says, "My people are destroyed for lack of knowledge." However, the opposite is also true; if you have knowledge you will not be destroyed.

Choose Who Should Lay Hands on You

The sum total of what I am saying is this: You will either influence other people or other people will influence you with their spirit.

Let me illustrate my point a little differently. Let us assume that you are in a small room, and this room is full of men smoking cigars, yet you yourself do not smoke. If you choose to stay in that room full of cigar smoke, you will smell with cigar smoke just like the men who smoked.

The transference of spirit is the same as transference of smoke; that is why it is so vital for every one of us to know those with whom we associate.

You must always be humble and prayerful in laying on hands. This does not mean you lay hands only on those who are clean. There was a time in my ministry when I did not want to touch a certain person. I did not want to put my hands on him. He was filthy. As a matter of fact, when he walked into the meeting I secretly hoped the ushers would kick him out. He was a transient.

196

He smelled bad. The whole room stank as soon as he walked in. He sat in the front row and smoked a rolled cigarette. Finally he got the hint, put it out and stuck it behind his ear. Flies buzzed around him, and he had lice on his clothing.

During the teaching I had difficulty concentrating. The smell, the lice, the flies and especially the cigarette were bothering me. It was just eating at me. Then God began to talk to me. He said, "Would you feel the same way about someone who came in well dressed and smelling good?" I said, "Well, no, Lord. That's a different situation." The Lord said, "That's what you were like when I got hold of you. I was smelling good, and you were smelling bad, yet I loved you. How dare you not love the soul that is in him! You are looking at outward things."

When I gave an invitation, this man stepped up and said, "Can I be saved?" God broke me, and I wept. When he accepted the Lord, I didn't see his lice. I didn't see his flies. I didn't smell his odor. I put my arms around him and prayed with him. The man was totally different when I looked at him with the eyes of Jesus rather than my natural eyes. He came back that afternoon. Although this man slept in the back of a car, he had somehow found a razor and a faucet. When he went back to his car, he tried to smoke a cigarette and got sick. He said, "I don't know what happened to me, but I just couldn't smoke anymore."

He was a different man. When God comes into your life, it transforms you. As a minister of God, let His love flow out of you. Lay hands on those whom He tells you to regardless of what they look like outwardly. Your love for them will cause the change that needs to take place.

If I had not gone to that man, perhaps he never would have felt what it is like to have someone embrace him. I had to put myself aside.

When you minister, do not be afraid to put hands on a person who has an open wound or skin disease. The blood of Jesus Christ is stronger. Sometimes, if you allow it, doubt comes in. "What if I catch it?" you say. You will catch it if that is your thought. Stand in the assurance and knowledge that when you lay on hands, the power of God in you will be stronger than the power of the disease and let the flow of God go through you into their bodies.

Let me give you an illustration. Most people, when they go into a hospital, are somewhat fearful. They do not want to catch any diseases. Doctors and nurses who are there day in and day out do not get sick. They do not catch diseases from the patients because they know what they are dealing with. Knowledge gives you strength and ability, and you will not be afraid.

You don't have to be afraid when someone puts their arms around you in a simple gesture of friendliness. But you should know a person before you lay on hands. Be cautious when you are seeking spiritual awareness and spiritual input. Not everyone who says, "Lord, Lord," is serving the Lord Jesus Christ.

Do not be intimidated because people come to you and say, "What kind of minister are you that you wouldn't go and pray for so-and-so?" That is nothing but a spirit of intimidation. Be like Jesus was when Martha and Mary said, "Oh, thy friend Lazarus is dying. As a matter of fact, he is dead." Jesus did not jump because someone told Him to go and pray. He went only when God said to go. Are you going to be influenced by people or are you going to be influenced by the Holy Spirit? If God tells you to lay hands on someone, He will honor your obedience. The power in you is greater than the power of the devil. If God says, "Don't touch them," do not put your hands on them. There is danger not only in the spirit but in the natural as well.

Don't Let the Sin Be Transferred to You

By laying on hands unprotected you can be a partaker. If you receive a negative spirit, it may be dormant for a long time. Then it will start manifesting itself. If the person you laid hands on had bursitis, you may feel a little uncomfortable in your shoulders or joints. The next day it may get a little worse. Before long you have to go to the doctor, and he gives you a prescription for bursitis. If a spirit enters in and you do not rebuke it immediately, then it has a place to dwell. You need not be afraid of this when you pray for someone.

Turn to Psalm 24. God desires that we, as believers, have clean hands. God is not going to receive anyone who has dirty hands or whose heart is not pure. For us to minister on God's behalf, our hands and heart must be pure and clean.

If your soul (your mind) is right, your hands will also be right. You cannot think wrongly and have clean hands. You cannot think about God's Word and have dirty hands. God demands of His children clean hands and a pure heart. Unlike those under the Old Testament, we have the blood of Christ, and when we come to Him and repent of our sins, He honors us.

Leviticus 4:13-15 says, "And if the whole congregation of Israel sin through ignorance, and the thing be hid from the eyes of the assembly, and they have done somewhat against any of the commandments of the Lord concerning things which should not be done, and are guilty; When the sin, which they have sinned against it, is known, then the congregation shall offer a young bullock for the sin, and bring him before the tabernacle of the congregation. And the elders of the congregation shall lay their hands upon the head of the bullock before the Lord: and the bullock shall be killed before the Lord."

Why didn't they put their hands upon the feet? Why didn't they put their hands on the tail? Why didn't they put their hands on the body? Why the head? Maybe you have never asked the question. It is the head that tells the tail to wiggle. It is the head that tells the feet to go. It is the head that tells the body what to do. That's why it is important for you to realize that your mind, your thoughts, will determine what your body will do. I am convinced that if you start believing and confessing what God says concerning you, you can speak yourself to health. I believe we can speak ourselves to prosperity. I believe we can speak ourselves to perfection with God. I believe we can speak ourselves to joy simply because when the head is confessing, the feet will follow. Proverbs 23:7 says, "For as he thinks in his heart so is he."

Even Mary, the mother of Jesus, said, "My soul (that's the head part) doth magnify the Lord." How many times have you been in a congregation and thought, "Why aren't these people lifting their hands and shouting? If God is God, why aren't they more joyful?" The head tells them not to be. They are ashamed and embarrassed for people to see them lifting their hands. Their spirits are rejoicing in God their Savior, but their heads say, "No, you don't want to be a fanatic. After all, you're a businessman. You're dignified." Pride comes in.

This is why King Saul's daughter, David's wife, was embarrassed. She wasn't embarrassed for David. She was embarrassed for herself. Do you know why? The Bible says that David danced before the Lord naked. You and I know that David would not literally dance naked. What David did was take off his royal robe. Then the garments which covered his flesh were just like the garments everybody wore. He became like them. You could not tell the difference between the king and the commoner. When she saw him do that, she said, "How could you be common?" With God we are all equal. When you are a child of God and your spirit starts rejoicing, you don't care what anybody thinks. The only ones who care are those who allow their heads and pride to rule them more than the spirit. David allowed his spirit to magnify the Lord and rejoice before God. He did not care what anybody thought about him. He just worshipped God.

"And the elders of the congregation shall lay their hands upon the head of the bullock before the Lord." By doing this the elders identified the sins of the congregation with the animal about to be slain. Romans 6:23 says, "For the wages of sin is death." When hands were laid on the animal by the elders, it was an act of transmitting, or transferring, the sin of the entire nation to a sinless, innocent animal. The innocent one died for the guilty.

That is why we can say, "He who knew no sin became sin for us, that we might become the righteousness of God in Christ." His blood not only covered our sin; it washed it away. We see that "all have sinned and come short of the glory of God" (Rom. 3:23). The wages of sin is death; therefore, by the laying on of hands we transmit the power of God. When you lay hands on people, there must be no question about whether you have clean hands and a pure heart. When you lay hands on people, you release yourself for the power to flow into them. As long as you keep your hands on them, the power will flow. There will be enough power to set them free if you continue generating the power within you. If you do not you can be drained of power. Mark 4 tells us that as soon as the seed is sown, the devil comes immediately to steal the Word.

When Christ was betrayed, He was betrayed into the hands of sinners. Jesus said, "For the prince of this world cometh, but he has nothing in me." The Word does not say He was betrayed into the *feet* of sinners. It says into the *hands* of sinners. When they caught Him, they put their hands on Him. To do what? To transmit their sin to Him. Jesus willingly accepted sin and took it to the cross and nailed it there. He allowed Himself to take our guilt and sin.

There were times when people tried to put hands on Jesus and He just walked through the crowd. When His time had come, however, He became the Lamb of God. John testified in John 1:29, "Behold the Lamb of God, which taketh away the sin of the world."

He is no longer the Lamb of God. He is the Son of the living God. He was the Lamb before He was slain. Matthew 26:21-24 says, "And as they did eat, [Jesus] said, Verily I say unto you, that one of you shall betray me. And they were exceeding sorrowful, and began every one of them to say unto him, Lord, is it I? And he answered and said, He that dippeth his hand with me in the dish, the same shall betray me. The Son of man goeth as it is written of him: but woe unto that man by whom the Son of man is betrayed! it had been good for that man if he had not been born."

201

Matthew 27:1-4 says, "When the morning was come, all the chief priests and elders of the people took counsel against Jesus to put him to death: And when they had bound him, they led him away, and delivered him to Pontius Pilate the governor. Then Judas, which had betrayed him, when he saw that he was condemned, repented himself, and brought again the thirty pieces of silver to the chief priests and elders, Saying, I have sinned in that I have betrayed the innocent blood."

Judas had no intention of killing Jesus. He loved Him. The flesh got in the way. When he saw the money and the oil, he thought it was being wasted. He was not thinking of the poor. He was thinking of himself. That's when the devil got hold of him and began to work on him. It all happened in the spirit realm. He confessed that he betrayed innocent blood. Matthew 27:23 says, "And the governor said, Why, what evil hath he done? But they cried out the more, saying, Let him be crucified."

The religious leaders wanted His blood to be shed; they wanted to crucify Him.

"When Pilate saw that he could prevail nothing, but that rather a tumult was made, he took water, and washed his hands before the multitude, saying, I am innocent of the blood of this just person: see ye to it" (v. 24).

When our hands are dirty, we take soap and water and wash them. We want to purify ourselves. Pilate said, "I will have nothing to do with this." He took water and washed his hands.

The psalmist says in Psalm 140:1, 4, "Deliver me, O Lord, from the evil man: preserve me from the violent man;...Keep me, O Lord, from the hands of the wicked; preserve me from the violent man; who have purposed to overthrow my goings."

Psalm 144:7-8 says, "Send thine hand from above; rid me, and deliver me out of great waters, from the hand of strange children; whose mouth speaketh vanity, and their right hand is a right hand of falsehood."

God honors those who have clean hands. In Acts 8, power is transmitted by the laying on of hands.

Acts 8:12-17 says: "But when they believed Philip preaching the things concerning the kingdom of God, and the name of Jesus Christ, they were baptized, both men and women. Then Simon himself believed also: and when he was baptized, he continued with Philip, and wondered, beholding the miracles and signs which were done. Now when the apostles which were at Jerusalem heard that Samaria had received the word of God, they sent unto them Peter and John: Who, when they were come down, prayed for them, that they might receive the Holy Ghost: (For as yet he was fallen upon none of them: only they were baptized in the name of the Lord Jesus.) Then laid they their hands on them, and they received the Holy Ghost."

It is obvious that before hands were laid on them, they received Christ. When they heard Philip preach, they received and believed. Receiving Christ is Step One. Receiving the Holy Spirit is Step Two. It does not say that Peter and John laid hands on them to receive Christ. When the apostles heard that Samaria had believed in Jesus Christ, they sent Peter and John to lay hands on the people so that they would receive the Holy Spirit.

It is very clear to me that before hands were laid upon them, the Holy Spirit was not transmitted to them. "And when Simon saw that through the laying on of the apostles' hands the Holy Ghost was given, he offered them money" (v. 18).

The evidence was real. Simon was a sorcerer before he became a believer. He knew the supernatural. The supernatural power he witnessed was far greater than any sorcery. It was so powerful, in fact, that he wanted to buy it. Peter rebuked him. You do not have to pay a price for it. It is a gift of God.

"And when Simon saw that through laying on of the apostles' hands the Holy Ghost was given, he offered them money, Saying, Give me also this power, that on whomsoever I lay hands, he may receive the Holy Ghost. But Peter said unto him, Thy money perish with thee, because thou hast thought that the gift of God may be purchased with money" (vv. 18-20). Peter rebuked him on the spot. When a brother or sister does something wrong, they must be corrected immediately. Do not be afraid of hurting their feelings. You are not trying to win a popularity contest. You are there to represent God.

In Hebrews 6:2 Paul says, "Of the doctrine of baptisms, and of laying on of hands, and of resurrection of the dead, and of eternal judgment." Whatever doctrine Christ gives us is a good doctrine. Anything that the Word of God has to offer we should receive gladly. If we do not have understanding, we have the Holy Spirit who teaches us all things.

The Holy Spirit will not keep anything secret from you if your motive is right. The Holy Spirit is here to teach you and show you what God has given you. That is why Jesus said, "I must go. If I don't go, the Comforter will not come. When He comes, He will guide you into all truth, for He is the Spirit of Truth." If you want to know what truth is, know the Word and ask the Spirit of God to help you.

CHAPTER FIFTEEN

Living the Spirit-Controlled Life

Many traditions of men have been brought into churches where, for lack of teaching, people believe that when they are born again they are free from all demonic attacks. This is completely false. If anything, demonic attacks increase. You will be more aware of demonic attacks than ever before because of the knowledge of the truth and your ability to discern. In 2 Corinthians 4:8-9 Paul tells us, "We are troubled on every side, yet not distressed; we are perplexed, but not in despair; persecuted, but not forsaken; cast down, but not destroyed."

I do not want to name any particular denomination, but I have been turned off by some of the methods in which people believe the Spirit should be transferred, especially to those seeking the baptism of the Holy Spirit. Many people have the idea that if you do not jerk the Spirit of God is not working through you. That is simply the flesh trying to get attention. Often they will say, "This is how my grandmother did it and my mother also. This is how we used to do it in our church."

Christians see these things and hear what so-and-so did. It may even be repulsive to them at first, but if they see and hear it long enough, they will follow the pattern. That is why it is so important to remember that, whatever you are doing, people are watching you. You may not think so, but they are watching you.

The Sons of God Are Led by the Spirit of God

The Spirit is available to every believer. You do not have to have a jerky head and shaky hands for the power of God to flow. I had a difficult time with this when I first asked people to lay hands on me to receive the baptism of the Holy Spirit. I didn't know whether I would come away from that place with my life. One person got hold of my neck, another got hold of my head, someone grabbed my shoulders and I was being pulled in all directions. I was a brand-new Christian. I did not know that this was just their tradition. They went through it the same way every time. That was how they received, so they wanted me to receive the same way. It stopped me from receiving.

The Holy Spirit is gentle. If you lay hands on someone, lay hands on them gently. Just barely touch them so it will not be a point of concentration. If you start jerking someone's head around, how are they going to concentrate on receiving (especially if they wear false teeth or a wig)? It's funny, but it's also a tragedy that through generations we have passed on erroneous traditions that have caused a lot of people to get turned off and say, "Who needs that?" That's what I said. I did not want to do what they were doing. In my mind and in my heart I knew it was not right, but I did not know the Scriptures. Why would God do that to His people?

The Holy Spirit is a gentleman. He will never force Himself on you. He will never shake you. When the Holy Spirit wants to use someone, the gifts will become manifest. Sometimes a person feels he is shaking on the inside. The Holy Spirit is energizing him, wanting him to yield, but the person holds back that power because of the fear he will not do it right or that it is not really the Spirit of the Lord. It's like a water hose with the faucet turned on and the nozzle barely open.

A person who is full of the Holy Spirit will sometimes have this experience inwardly. The Holy Spirit is gently prodding him to open up so the power will flow. Usually this happens when the person is new at the operation of spiritual gifts and does not know exactly how to move in the Spirit. When you yield to the Holy Spirit and He has freedom to move through you, the inward experience moves outward. The longer you walk in the Spirit, the easier it is for the Spirit of God to flow. When God tells you to give a prophecy, you prophesy. When God speaks, you hear His voice and deliver the message. There is no resistance within you.

The Spirit of God always desires to use the believer in anointing and the operation of miracles. God wants us to operate in miracles so we can be a channel for Him to flow through. God needs us.

God Leads, the Devil Pushes

On the other hand, the spirit of the world causes feelings of rejection and the need for attention, self-edification, self-exaltation or self-accomplishments. Spirits of the world also desire a place in which to dwell and do their work.

The devil knows that when you see things, your flesh will desire them. Let's use popcorn as an example. You walk into a theater and smell popcorn. You immediately have to have a bag of it. It is not good enough just to have a bag of popcorn; it has to have a lot of butter and salt on it. Then you want a candy bar and a Coke also.

The devil concentrates on your weaknesses. There is a potato chip commercial that says, "No one can eat just one." When you taste one chip, all of a sudden your whole system goes into gear and you have to have one more and then another. Before you know it, the whole bag is gone. The devil uses the five senses to manipulate. He tries to get you addicted so that a habit will control you.

The devil knows when we are weak and when we are strong. As long as we are full of the Word, he will stay away from us. The Bible says the devil will depart for a season. A season could be a year or two. It could be a lifetime. The length of the season does not depend on the devil; it depends on you. You stay in season twenty-four hours a day all of your life by being full of the Word. Do that, and the devil will run from you. I did not say there wouldn't be obstacles, but you will be so full of the Holy Spirit and power that those obstacles will not even be a challenge to you. You will just step right over them.

An ant is a nuisance, but I am not afraid of ants. I will step right on top of them. They are not a challenge to me. I will step on the whole anthill. When you are full of God's Spirit, the devil and his demons are nothing but a bunch of ants. You will be able to walk all over them. Why? Because you are walking in faith and power.

The Bible says if you are given to appetite it would be better for you to cut your throat than to give yourself to the lusts of the flesh.

Sexual perversion is a very powerful spirit. Sex is not bad. God said it is good. However, the devil tries to pervert everything that is good. If we are perverted in a sexual area, we will perform abnormal sexual acts. Likewise, food is good and essential. The devil knows we need food. Without food we will die. He perverts it and causes us to lust after food.

The prophet Eli was not a sexually immoral man. His sons were. They had a sexual perversion and were permitting sexual acts in the sanctuary. Where do you suppose they got that from? They got it from their father. Why? Because Eli had a lust for food. He was so heavy that when he fell he broke his neck. He could not even walk! What difference does it make how you die? Does it make a difference if you die of food perversion or sexual perversion?

All of these areas—seeing, hearing, tasting, touching and smelling—must be under control. The Spirit of God must be in control, not only of our spirit but also of our fleshly desires. The devil knows the weakness of the flesh. When a person is truly born again, his spirit does not belong to the devil. The Bible says the wicked one touches him not (see 1 John 5:18). However, you must deal with your flesh.

The devil cannot control your mind unless you give it to him. He cannot come into your life and control it unless you allow him to. If most Christians were to see the devil coming down the road as a roaring lion, saying, "I am going to tempt you with food," they would say, "No, devil! I'm in control of my stomach. You are not going to tempt me with food." But the devil does not come as a roaring lion in a red suit with a briefcase. He comes as a thief, very subtly, and says, "Well, that's really not so bad, is it?"

I try to be protective of people in our church. I want to know where they go, who they listen to and what they read. Why? My responsibility is to watch over them, teach them and train them. When you listen to someone who claims to be a man of God, what is going to happen if you are deceived and that person lays hands on you?

Let's say this person has a spirit of homosexuality. You say, "A Christian homosexual?" The person has yielded himself willingly to that spirit. He may teach, preach and speak well. But when you allow yourself to open up to that spirit, not knowing the person or his fruit, you are vulnerable to that spirit.

If a man of God in leadership allows the spirit of the world to operate through his five senses, sooner or later it is going to manifest through him and out of his mouth to the congregation. The Bible says that out of the abundance of the heart the mouth speaks. Think what is going to happen to the brand-new lambs who are in the congregation. You are feeding them. Whatever comes out of you, they are going to believe.

Make sure you test the spirits. Make sure you listen to every word that is said, how it is said and what kind of motives are there to determine what kind of spirit is in control. A person may preach a good message, but what is their lifestyle? What kind of example are they? Do they fear God twenty-four hours a day or only when others are watching? It is your responsibility to find out. The Bible says to test the spirits.

I am just as vulnerable as anybody else. I am just as open to these things as anyone else. I choose not to give in to them. That is my choice. I choose to serve God. I choose to keep my eyes on Jesus. We are all vulnerable.

A man of God who receives the anointing and power has the ability to shut off his fleshly appetites of the five senses and yield himself to the Holy Spirit. Rather than being yielded to the world, his five senses will be yielded to the Holy Spirit.

When he is anointed, he is able to perceive things in the Spirit. His smell, touch and hearing become attuned to the Spirit of God. He is able to hear as God speaks to him. He is able to smell the presence of God. He is able to touch God with his spiritual hands. He is able to reach out and touch God's people and transmit power to them. God's power will flow because he yields himself to the Spirit.

Because the devil uses the flesh and the flesh is unredeemed, we have to cope with it and learn. Instead of reacting to jabs of the devil, we learn to shut them off and say, "No, devil, man shall not live by bread alone, but by every word of God. I'm a child of God. I yield all of my senses to the Holy Spirit for Him to use me."

Always ask God whether you should lay hands on someone and whether you should pray with them. It is not always advisable to go and preach at a particular place just because someone wants you to come. We must go only when the Holy Spirit bids us go. Let the Holy Spirit lead you, rather than the other way around.

First Corinthians 4:18-20 says, "Now some are puffed up, as

though I would not come to you. But I will come to you shortly, if the Lord will, and will know, not the speech of them which are puffed up, but the power. For the kingdom of God is not in word, but in power."

Many people use this passage as a scapegoat to explain why they do not want to do certain things. The timing of God is important. God does not want any to perish. It is the will of God that all be saved, but all are not saved. God wills that everybody be healthy, but not everybody is healthy. God wills that all prosper, but not everybody is prospering. Not everyone wants to be saved or be baptized in the Holy Spirit.

People have a choice to make. You cannot force healing upon them. You cannot force salvation upon them. You cannot force the baptism of the Holy Spirit on them. When they decide, there is no stopping them. I am going to go where the Holy Spirit leads me and not where I lead Him, because I do not want to be where the Holy Spirit is not.

When you follow the Holy Spirit, you never have to be concerned how it is going to turn out. The Holy Spirit never misses. When you lay hands on someone in response to God's prompting, you don't have to be afraid that a spirit is going to jump on you. God in you is greater than that spirit!

Many individuals who have tasted the Word of God and known the power of God have yet turned away and become hardened. They have chosen to go in a different direction.

How can that be? The lust of the flesh and the pride of life give pleasure for a season. Their minds have been seared with a hot iron, and they are no longer able to hear God. They hear another spirit and are convinced that it is real. The devil gives them supernatural revelation, and they turn away from God just like the prophet Baal.

According to Hebrews 6:1, certain doctrines are part of the foundation of the church: the doctrine of baptism, the resurrection of the dead, the eternal judgment, the repentance from dead works and faith toward God in the laying on of hands.

In the Old Testament the laying on of hands in consecration imparted power. Likewise, when we impart God's power, we have the ability to impart that power into people's lives, for good or bad. It is important for us always to be in tune with the Holy Spirit regarding how we conduct ourselves.

CHAPTER SIXTEEN

How Spirits Influence Humans

A s previously stated, there are basically three spirits with which we deal: the Spirit of God, the spirit of the world and the spirit of man. These spirits influence human beings in different ways.

Romans 10:15 says, "And how shall they preach, except they be sent?" How will the world know unless someone sends a preacher? In essence, when we are filled with God's Spirit, we become God's mouthpiece. If this is true, then the opposite is true also. Human beings can be filled with the wrong spirit. They become the devil's mouthpiece when they speak what the world says rather than what God says. You and I need to draw a line in our minds and not allow anything of the world to come in from the other side. We have the power to do that.

One of the areas we are discussing is the laying on of hands. In the Old Testament the laying on of hands was done in consecration, in blessing or for the inheritance of a blessing.

Genesis 27:15-26 says: "And Rebekah took goodly raiment of her eldest son Esau, which were with her in the house, and put them upon Jacob her younger son: And she put the skins of the kids of the goats upon his hands, and upon the smooth of his neck: And she gave the savoury meat and the bread, which she had prepared, into the hand of her son Jacob. And he came unto his father, and said, My father: and he said, Here am I; who art thou, my son? And Jacob said unto his father, I am Esau thy firstborn; I have done according as thou badest me: arise, I pray thee, sit and eat of my venison, that thy soul may bless me. And Isaac said unto his son, How is it that thou hast found it so quickly, my son? And he said, Because the Lord thy God brought it to me. And Isaac said unto Jacob, Come near, I pray thee, that I may feel thee, my son, whether thou be my very son Esau or not. And Jacob went near unto Isaac his father; and he felt him, and said, The voice is Jacob's voice, but the hands are the hands of Esau. And he discerned him not, because his hands were hairy, as his brother Esau's hands: so he blessed him. And he said, Art thou my very son Esau? And he said, I am. And he said, Bring it near to me, and I will eat of my son's venison, that my soul may bless thee. And he brought it near to him, and he did eat: and he brought him wine, and he drank. And his father Isaac said unto him, Come near now, and kiss me, my son."

"And he came near, and kissed him: and he smelled the smell of his raiment..." (v. 27). Isaac knew something was not right, but he could not put his finger on it. Isaac's vision was poor, so he could not see. "And he came near, and kissed him: and he smelled the smell of his raiment, and blessed him, and said, See, the smell of my son is as the smell of a field which the Lord hath blessed: Therefore God give thee of the dew of heaven, and the fatness of the earth, and plenty of corn and wine: Let people serve thee, and nations bow down to thee: be lord over thy brethren, and let thy mother's sons bow down to thee: cursed be every one that curseth thee, and blessed by he that blesseth thee" (vv. 27-29).

Why would the mother would get involved in such a deception? Surely if she was the mother of both Esau and Jacob, she should not have a preference of one over the other. Mothers are not any different today than they were then.

"And it came to pass, as soon as Isaac had made an end of blessing Jacob, and Jacob was yet scarce gone out from the presence of Isaac his father, that Esau his brother came in from his hunting. And he also had made savoury meat, and brought it unto his father, and said unto his father, Let my father arise, and eat of his son's venison, that thy soul may bless me" (vv. 30-31).

The words that Jacob used, Esau was using as well. Apparently he must have heard his older brother use this terminology before. "And Isaac his father said unto him, Who art thou?" These are the same words he said to Jacob. He is not distressed, and maybe even confused at this point. "And he said, I am thy son, thy first-born Esau" (v. 32).

When deception takes place, confusion follows. Isaac does not know exactly what has transpired. The Bible says that where confusion is, there are evil works. You do not want to be confused. You do not want to be deceived when you go and lay hands on people. You must know exactly what you are doing. You do not want to fall into a trap.

"And Isaac trembled very exceedingly, and said, Who? where is he that hath taken venison, and brought it me, and I have eaten of all before thou camest, and have blessed him? yea, and he shall be blessed" (v. 33).

Once he had blessed Jacob he could not retrieve it. The blessing went into the person upon whom it was pronounced.

"And when Esau heard the words of his father, he cried with a great and exceeding bitter cry, and said unto his father, Bless me, even me also, O my father. And he said, Thy brother came with subtilty, and hath taken away thy blessing" (vv. 34-35).

Those who come to deceive can drain your spiritual power if you allow them to get near you and put hands on you. You have to protect yourself.

"And he said, Thy brother came with subtilty, and hath taken away thy blessing. And he said, Is not he rightly named Jacob? for he hath supplanted me these two times" (vv. 35-36).

Even at the moment they were born, the Bible says Esau came first, and Jacob held on to his heel.

"And he said, Is he not rightly named Jacob? for he hath supplanted me these two times: he took away my birthright; and, behold, now he hath taken away my blessing. And he said, Hast thou not reserved a blessing for me?" (v. 36).

How did Jacob take the birthright? Let's look at Genesis 25:27-28: "And the boys grew: and Esau was a cunning hunter, a man of the field; and Jacob was a plain man, dwelling in tents. And Isaac loved Esau, because he did eat of his venison: but Rebekah loved Jacob."

You scratch my back, I'll scratch yours. You fill my belly, I'll fill yours. Jacob was a peaceable young man. He was around the house. He was not always hunting. Apparently Isaac was out in the field as well and saw Esau's skillfulness. To this day a father likes a boy who is athletic. He is drawn to that son, while his other son may be more inclined to read. A father really doesn't want to have anything to do with a young boy who sits there with glasses on, thin and frail-looking, reading a book. The father wants a "real boy." We see an example right here. Even though Isaac was a man of God, he had a feeling for the older more than the younger. That tells me the younger was not as outgoing as the older.

Because Jacob hung around the house and the father and the older brother were not there, the mother grew fonder of the younger son. There was a mutual relationship. The mother needed someone to show her love to just as much as the child did. Since the father was not there and the mother was, Jacob was closer to the mother.

Rebekah should have been a mother to both the older and the younger, but because the younger was closer to her, she loved him more. You may have two or three children, but perhaps there's a special one, and you give that child just a little bit extra. This special relationship caused Rebekah to push her son to be blessed. She knew the importance of the blessing. It happened not only in this situation, but also with the sons of Zebedee when the mother said to Jesus, "I would like for one of my sons to sit on your right hand, and one to sit on your left hand. All these other guys are OK, but my sons are special." We see favoritism at work. Subtlety and deception came in, and Rebekah put her favorite son in a position to be blessed.

"And Jacob sod [boiling] pottage: and Esau came from the field, and he was faint: And Esau said to Jacob, Feed me, I pray thee, with that same red pottage; for I am faint" (Gen. 25:29-30). Apparently Jacob also knew how to cook. Esau had eaten this red pottage before, and he knew what it tasted like. When the red pottage was being boiled, he said, "Feed me with the same red pottage that you did before."

"And Esau said to Jacob, Feed me, I pray thee, with that same red pottage; for I am faint: therefore was his name called Edom [red]. And Jacob said, Sell me this day thy birthright" (vv. 30-31). Remember Esau said, "He has cheated me twice. He cheated me out of my birthright. He's cheating me out of my blessing." You can now see the anger welling up within him. He is getting upset.

Jacob was an opportunist. He was looking for a chance to advance himself. There was division, and their parents were the models.

We see Jacob saying to his brother, "Sell me this day thy birthright. And Esau said, Behold, I am at the point to die: and what profit shall this birthright do to me?" (vv. 31-32). Esau was convinced he was going to die if he did not get something to eat.

He said, "What good is my birthright going to do me if I'm dead?" Doesn't the world say, "Eat, drink and be merry, for tomorrow you may die"? You can see the world manifesting in him. It is a carnal spirit. Getting the food was more important to Esau than believing God. Esau was willing. Jacob did not force him.

"And Jacob said, Swear to me this day; and he sware unto him: and he sold his birthright unto Jacob. Then Jacob gave Esau bread and pottage of lentiles; and he did eat and drink, and rose up, and went his way: thus Esau despised his birthright" (vv. 33-34).

In chapter 27 Esau is accusing Jacob of stealing both his birthright and his blessing. In fact, Esau was the one who allowed it to happen.

Genesis 27:37-41 says, "And Isaac answered and said unto Esau, Behold, I have made him thy lord, and all his brethren have I given to him for servants; and with corn and wine have I sustained him: and what shall I do now unto thee, my son? And Esau said unto his father, Hast thou but one blessing, my father? bless me, even me also, O my father. And Esau lifted up his voice, and wept. And Isaac his father answered and said unto him, Behold, thy dwelling shall be the fatness of the earth, and of the dew of heaven from above; and by thy sword shalt thou live, and shalt serve thy brother; and it shall come to pass when thou shalt have the dominion, that thou shalt break his yoke from off thy neck. And Esau hated Jacob because of the blessing wherewith his father blessed him: and Esau said in his heart, The days of mourning for my father are at hand; then will I slay my brother Jacob."

Chapter 28:1-4 says, "And Isaac called Jacob, and blessed him, and charged him, and said unto him, Thou shalt not take a wife of the daughters of Canaan." Canaan was the land that God promised. Its people were enemies of God's people. "Arise, go to Padanaram, to the house of Bethuel thy mother's father; and take thee a wife from thence of the daughters of Laban thy mother's brother. And God Almighty bless thee, and make thee fruitful, and multiply thee, that thou mayest be a multitude of people. And give thee the blessing of Abraham, to thee, and to thy seed with thee; that thou mayest inherit the land wherein thou art a stranger, which God gave unto Abraham."

"When Esau saw that Isaac had blessed Jacob, and sent him away to Padanaram to take him a wife from thence; and that as he blessed him he gave him a charge, saying, Thou shalt not take a wife of the daughters of Canaan; and that Jacob obeyed his father and his mother, and was gone to Padanaram; and Esau seeing that the daughters of Canaan pleased not Isaac his father; then went Esau unto Ishmael, and took unto the wives which he had Mahalath the daughter of Ishmael Abraham's son, the sister of Nebajoth, to be his wife. And Jacob went out from Beersheba, and went toward Haran" (vv. 6-10).

Rebellion took hold in Esau because of the family relationship. Esau knew his father told Jacob not to take a wife from the Canaanites, so he disobeyed his father, knowing it would displease him. Because he went against his father, he went against God. Esau sold his birthright, blaming Jacob, and the rebellion has continued from that day. Look at Lebanon, Syria and the Arabs. They are still fighting among themselves because the rebellious spirit that entered them then is still at large.

False Teachers Deceive and lead People Astray

In Genesis 48 Joseph requested that Jacob lay hands upon his sons. Jacob became Israel. That was his new name, but he was still Jacob. Jacob was a man who used deception to get the blessing. Chapter 48:8-14 says, "And Israel beheld Joseph's sons, and said, Who are these? And Joseph said unto his father, They are my sons, whom God hath given me in this place. And he said, Bring them, I pray thee, unto me, and I will bless them. Now the eyes of Israel were dim for age, so that he could not see. And he brought them near unto him; and he kissed them, and embraced them. And Israel said unto Joseph, I had not thought to see thy face: and, lo, God hath shewed me also thy seed. And Joseph brought them out from between his knees, and he bowed himself with his face to the earth.

And Joseph took them both, Ephraim in his right hand toward Israel's left hand, and Manasseh in his left hand toward Israel's right hand, and brought them near unto him. And Israel stretched out his right hand, and laid it upon Ephraim's head, who was the younger, and his left hand upon Manasseh's head, guiding his hands wittingly; for Manasseh was the firstborn."

This story is really beautiful once we see what is taking place. Joseph is coming with a similar situation. Joseph, the son of Jacob, was taken by his brothers and sold into Egypt because of the revelation of God that he told to his brothers. They became angry. Anger was passed on to future generations from the fathers.

"And he blessed Joseph, and said, God, before whom my fathers Abraham and Isaac did walk, the God which fed me all my life long unto this day, the Angel which redeemed me from all evil, bless the lads; and let my name be named on them, and the name of my fathers Abraham and Isaac; and let them grow into a multitude in the midst of the earth. And when Joseph saw that his father laid his right hand upon the head of Ephraim, it displeased him: and he held up his father's hand, to remove it from Ephraim's head unto Manasseh's head" (vv. 15-17).

Manasseh was the firstborn. Even though Israel was not able to see them, he knew by the Spirit what he wanted to do.

"And Joseph said unto his father, Not so, my father: for this is the firstborn; put thy right hand upon his head" (v. 18).

It was important which hand they put upon those who were firstborn to receive the blessing.

"And his father refused, and said, I know it, my son, I know it: he also shall become a people, and he also shall be great: but truly his younger brother shall be greater than he, and his seed shall become a multitude of nations" (v. 19).

Knowing the Truth Will Set You Free

Even though Israel was not able to see in the natural, he was able to perceive in the spirit upon whom to lay hands to bless and upon whom not to lay hands to bless, even though by right the firstborn was to be blessed. Because Israel perceived that Ephraim had a softer spirit than Manasseh, God allowed him to place his hands where he did. All of this looks like deception. Nevertheless, God looks on the heart. Jacob received the blessing because Esau was a man who was not seeking God. Jacob, because he was soft in heart, was seeking after spiritual things. He knew that even though he was to give the pottage to his brother, the birthright was worth more than one meal. God, knowing this, allowed the blessing to rest upon Jacob, who became Israel.

Be sensitive to the Spirit, and lay hands only upon those people whom the Spirit of God directs you to, so that the blessing will flow. If you have a check in your spirit, you will know it is not right. If you go ahead and disobey the check of the Spirit, before long you too will become spiritually deaf. You will no longer hear the still small voice speaking to you.

Do not lay hands on people just because you have been enticed to or to please mankind. You are here as servants of God to please God, and Him only, so that His blessing will flow. If you do not, the blessing of God will not flow. When the blessing of God does not flow, people are not healed. You may get discouraged. A lot of people have gone by the wayside simply because they were ministering in the flesh and not in the Spirit.

In Exodus 29:10 we see that it was important for the priest to lay hands upon an animal to transmit the sins of the people so the innocent could die for the guilty. Verses 18-20 say, "And thou shalt burn the whole ram upon the altar: it is a burnt offering unto the Lord: it is a sweet savour, an offering made by fire unto the Lord. And thou shalt take the other ram; and Aaron and his sons shall put their hands upon the head of the ram. Then shalt thou kill the ram, and take of his blood, and put it upon the tip of the right ear of Aaron, and upon the tip of the right ear of his sons, and upon the thumb of their right hand, and upon the great toe of their right foot, and sprinkle the blood upon the altar round about."

They needed to take the blood and put it on the earlobe, the thumb and the toe. This meant the ear was anointed to hear the Word of God, the hands to be an extension of God and the feet to take the message of God.

In Numbers 8:10-15 we see again the laying on of hands: "And thou shalt bring the Levites before the Lord: and the children of Israel shall put their hands on the Levites: And Aaron shall offer the Levites before the Lord for an offering of the children of Israel, that they may execute the service of the Lord.

"And the Levites shall lay their hands upon the heads of the bullocks: and thou shalt offer the one for a sin offering, and the other for a burnt offering, unto the Lord, to make an atonement for the Levites. And thou shalt set the Levites before Aaron, and before his sons and offer them for an offering unto the Lord. Thus shalt thou separate the Levites from among the children of Israel: and the Levites shall be mine. And after that shall the Levites go in to do the service of the tabernacle of the congregation: and thou shalt cleanse them, and offer them for an offering."

This was the preparation of the Levites—presenting them to the Lord, laying hands upon them, imparting the blessing of God and preparing them to become servants of the most high God.

Not only were they anointed for service, but they were offered to God. In the Old Testament as well as the New Testament the practice of laying on hands was used to ordain or to put a person before the Lord. By the laying on of hands, the anointing of God is imparted to the person to do the service of the Lord.

The Bible says that in the presence of the multitude, Moses took Joshua and laid hands upon him.

Numbers 27:15-18 says, "And Moses spake unto the Lord,

saying, Let the Lord, the God of the spirits of all flesh, set a man over the congregation, which may go out before them, and which may go in before them, and which may lead them out, and which may bring them in; that the congregation of the Lord be not as sheep which have no shepherd. And the Lord said unto Moses, Take thee Joshua the son of Nun, a man in whom is the spirit, and lay thine hand upon him."

The Bible says in Deuteronomy 34 that Moses placed his hand upon Joshua because God commanded him to do so. "And Moses was an hundred and twenty years old when he died: his eye was not dim, nor his natural force abated. And the children of Israel wept for Moses in the plains of Moab thirty days: so the days of weeping and mourning for Moses were ended. And Joshua the son of Nun was full of the spirit of wisdom; for Moses had laid his hands upon him: and the children of Israel hearkened unto him, and did as the Lord commanded Moses" (vv. 7-9).

Moses was gone. But when Moses obeyed God and did as He commanded, the spirit that God gave to Moses as a leader was transferred to Joshua. He received the wisdom, the understanding, the knowledge and the power. Everything that Moses had, God gave to Joshua by the laying on of hands and by transmitting the spirit that was upon Moses.

Numbers 27:19-23 says, "And set him before Eleazar the priest, and before all the congregation; and give him a charge in their sight. And thou shalt put some of thine honour upon him, that all the congregation of the children of Israel may be obedient. And he shall stand before Eleazar the priest, who shall ask counsel for him after the judgment of Urim before the Lord: at his word shall they go out, and at his word they shall come in, both he, and all the children of Israel with him, even all the congregation. And Moses did as the Lord commanded him: and he took Joshua, and set him before Eleazar the priest, and before all the congregation: And he laid his hands upon him, and gave him a charge, as the Lord commanded by the hand of Moses."

When God tells you to lay hands on the sick or to anoint people for His service, do it. You may not feel anything in your hands. You may not even feel well that day in the natural. It doesn't depend upon your perkiness. It depends upon your obedience. When we lay hands upon a person, God will do the rest.

When Moses laid hands upon Joshua, did something happen in Joshua's life? Was the ritual Moses performed effective? Yes. Deuteronomy 34:7-9 tells us Joshua received wisdom, power and authority that people recognized and obeyed.

How, then, was sin transferred from the people to the goats that were before the priests? How was sin transferred from the priests and the congregation? How were they able to transmit the sins of the congregation upon the innocent animals that were brought before them? By spitting on them? No. By blowing on them? No. By washing them with water? No. By christening them? No. How? *By laying on of hands!* Sin was transmitted from the guilty to the innocent by the laying on of hands.

How, then, did the sin of the world transfer to Jesus, who was sinless? He was perfect even though people touched Him. There were people who came and touched not only Him but also His garment. When people with needs came and touched Him, they were made whole.

The answer is, Jesus *became* sin for us. Our sin was transferred upon the sinless Lamb of God. John testifies of this in John 1:29.

Though Jesus was sinless, because of Adam's sin death came upon us all. Jesus came to take away that sin and to give us life eternal. He said the grace of God, the righteousness of God and the gift of God came that we might reign in life with Him. We then, by accepting Christ, will never die. As a matter of fact, whether you are a sinner or a believer you will never die. The difference is where you will spend eternity. You will either spend it in the presence of God or in the presence of Satan. The spirit is indestructible; it goes on living forever.

Jesus was sinless, yet He became sin for us that through His obedience and the price He paid, we might escape eternal hell and have instead eternal life.

CHAPTER SEVENTEEN

You Become What You Permit in Your Life

O n the earth Jesus lived without sin. The Bible says He became sin for us. He became the substitute for us so that we could take His place and be accepted by God as His children. Jesus paid the price.

Until Jesus was crucified, He was sinless. He was tempted in all areas as we are, and yet He was without sin. He knew every temptation and every suffering that a human being can experience.

When did the sin of mankind enter into Him? At what point did this happen? It is important for us to know how sin or a wrong spirit can be transferred even to a believer. If Jesus received sin and became sin for us, how can we prevent someone from putting their sin on us?

Remember what Paul said to Timothy: "Lay hands on no man suddenly, neither be partaker of other men's sins."

Before you become a partaker of another man's sin, you have to desire what he has and agree to whatever he is doing. If a person wants you to join him in robbing a bank, you have to say, "No, I do not want to do that because it is against the law." He may say, "Well, at least give me a ride to the bank and wait for me. You don't have to do anything." If you agree to any part of this you become an accomplice. You are as guilty as the person who actually committed the crime. You allowed yourself to be talked into participating. The sin of the person who robbed the bank is just as much yours.

When you become a companion to a person who is a sinner and allow him to influence you, you are agreeing to his sin. You become a part of that sin. If you stay around long enough, your conscience will be seared and you will no longer feel that the sins he commits are wrong.

Matthew 21:45-46 says, "And when the chief priests and Pharisees had heard his parables, they perceived that he spake of them. But when they sought to lay hands on him, they feared the multitude, because they took him for a prophet."

The Pharisees wanted to put their hands on Jesus. They wanted to do Him harm. It was their intent to transmit to Him their feelings of anger, frustration and dislike and deprive Him of that which He was doing because He was speaking the truth. They wanted to put their hands on Him, but they were afraid the people would turn against them. However, this is not the real reason they could not put their hands on Him.

We know that when Jesus was in the synagogue ministering, people laid their hands on Him. They touched Him. This was a different kind of touching from that which the Pharisees wanted to do. You need to see the difference so you will not wonder: What if I go to a meeting and people lay hands on me? Nothing will happen to you if they lay hands on you unless you are called for a specific ministry where you are appointed and anointed and the time has come for you to minister. When you are under the anointing, you have to be careful who lays hands on you. That is why I have people around me when I am ministering. I do not want anyone to sneak up behind me and lay hands on me. It has happened. It completely drained me and also made me physically sick. It took me two weeks to recover. The Lord showed me that I was not protecting myself. Having learned this the hard way, I am sharing it with you so you will not have to experience what I went through.

The Pharisees, Sadducees and priests would have loved to have been rid of Jesus. If they could have taken Him quietly and stuffed Him in a hole somewhere, they would have done it. They could not touch Him. Why?

John 7:28-30 says, "Then cried Jesus in the temple as he taught, saying, Ye both know me, and ye know whence I am: and I am not come of myself, but he that sent me is true, whom ye know not. But I know him: for I am from him, and he hath sent me. Then they sought to take him: but no man laid hands on him, because his hour was not yet come."

Wherever Jesus was people touched Him, but the intent of the Pharisees was to get rid of Him. The Pharisees could not get hold of Him because they were afraid of what the multitudes would do to them. The real truth was that they could not get hold of Him because His hour was not yet come. God kept them away. The devil wanted to destroy Him from the day He was born, and he tried to. Herod sent a multitude of soldiers and killed two thousand young children, wanting to destroy Jesus before He became a man. The Holy Spirit kept the devil and all those people away from Him. They could not transmit unto Him what they desired to transmit. When your time is not up, God is able to keep you in all things, and the devil will not touch you.

In Matthew 26 we see how Jesus knew His time had come, almost like a woman who is pregnant. She goes through the pregnancy, and when her hour is about to come she senses that she will soon have the baby. She is alerted by certain pains and symptoms that occur in her body. It is the same in the spirit realm as well. In the spirit realm you also sense and feel. Sometimes you even feel pain within you. Jesus was grieved in the Spirit. He wept. He perceived in His Spirit that the hour was about to come upon Him. He even asked the Father, if it was possible, to let it pass Him by. But He recognized that no one else could give birth when He was the one who was "pregnant." Another woman cannot give birth to your child if you are pregnant. You are the only one who can do it. This is just as true in the spirit realm.

It was not a Pharisee or Sadducee who betrayed Him. It was one of His own. Even though Judas Iscariot had tremendous responsibility, he had a weakness. The devil does not come through your strength but through your weakness.

Matthew 26:22-23 says, "And they were exceeding sorrowful, and began every one of them to say unto him, Lord, is it I? And he answered and said, He that dippeth his hand with me in the dish, the same shall betray me."

You may say, "I wouldn't have dipped anything. I would not even dare to get my hands out of my pockets. I would not even go near that dish." But the one who loves God yet is driven by a wrong spirit does not even realize he is dipping. He does not realize he is being led by a demonic spirit.

This wrong spirit comes into the body of Christ when people devour, criticize and blame those in spiritual authority over them. They blame everybody except themselves. Why? Because they are blinded by a wrong spirit. They are dipping their hand in the bowl and don't even know it. They are the ones who betray you. It is not you they hate but Jesus in you. Those who love God, who are sincere and pure in heart, will not dip in the dish of betrayal. But those who have evil motives and desires will dip. Let me show you why.

John 12:1-5 says, "Then Jesus six days before the passover came to Bethany, where Lazarus was which had been dead, whom he raised from the dead. There they made him a supper; and Martha served: but Lazarus was one of them that sat at the table with him. Then took Mary a pound of ointment of spikenard, very costly, and anointed the feet of Jesus, and wiped his feet with her hair: and the house was filled with the odour of the ointment. Then saith one of his disciples, Judas Iscariot, Simon's son, which should betray him, Why was not this ointment sold for three hundred pence, and given to the poor?"

Three hundred pence is approximately $45. At that time $45 was a considerable sum of money. The same spirit of greed that seized Judas is prevalent today.

Judas Iscariot was Jesus' disciple, but he was displeased with Jesus. He was angry with Him. The anger in his heart was not from heaven. Because of the circumstances, he did not think Mary should have done what she did.

Judas was expressing his frustration and anger. "This he said, *not that he cared for the poor; but because he was a thief*, and had the bag, and bare what was put therein. Then said Jesus, Let her alone: against the day of my burying hath she kept this. For the poor always ye have with you; but me ye have not always" (vv. 6-8, italics added).

When people condemn or criticize, they are not really concerned about anybody else. They are concerned about "me, myself and I."

Judas is saying, "Hey! I'm the treasurer. If you had sold that and put the money into the bag, I would have had more to steal." Money was Judas' weakness. There are babies in the church. We all love babies, but when babies have beards you hope they would act more like mature adults. People who get bent out of shape are those who say, "I want to do something, but you won't let me," or perhaps they are not willing to commit themselves.

The Bible says some are blessed thirtyfold, some sixtyfold, some one hundredfold. God is not a thirtyfold God. God is a one hundredfold God. Why are some blessed only thirtyfold?

231

Commitment. They are not willing to pay the price. Because they are not willing, they condemn you because they do not want to be alone in their weakness. They want to put their guilt trip on you as well.

A person will tell you he is committed, but his spirit is the same as Judas'. Such people think only about themselves. If they were honest they would tell you what the real problem is. The problem is not the pastor. The problem is them. They have the problem but they will use someone else as a scapegoat because their pride will not allow them to admit their problem. If they do, it means they have to roll up their sleeves and get involved. They do not want to do that. They want someone else to spoonfeed them and minister to them and feel sorry for them because they are full of self-pity.

It is not sin to have a weakness. It is sin not to admit your weakness and to allow the devil to use that weakness to destroy the body of Christ. Matthew 26 says, "Then cometh Jesus with them unto a place called Gethsemane, and saith unto the disciples, Sit ye here, while I go and pray yonder. And he took with him Peter and the two sons of Zebedee, and began to be sorrowful and very heavy. Then saith he unto them, My soul is exceeding sorrowful, even unto death: tarry ye here, and watch with me. And he went a little farther, and fell on his face, and prayed, saying, O my Father, if it be possible, let this cup pass from me: nevertheless, not as I will, but as thou wilt" (vv. 36-39). You can see the flesh and the spirit at war. Jesus knew why He came to earth, but His flesh was experiencing pain, sorrow and agony like a woman in travail just before birth. Jesus knew His time had come.

"And he cometh unto the disciples, and findeth them asleep, and saith unto Peter, What, could ye not watch with me one hour?" (v. 40).

Jesus was about to be crucified. He was about to be turned over to sinners, and Peter was asleep. Peter allowed his flesh to rule him. Verse 41 says, "Watch and pray, that ye enter not into temptation: the spirit indeed is willing, but the flesh is weak." You must not take your eyes off Jesus. You cannot take your eyes off the Word. You cannot go to sleep. If you do take your eyes off the Word (Jesus), you will fall into temptation. The thing that keeps you from temptation is watching and praying. When you are looking at Jesus, the temptation will not overcome you, because greater is He that is in you than he that is in the world.

To watch and pray means to keep looking to Jesus and to let the Word of God dwell in your heart richly.

"He went away again the second time, and prayed, saying, O my Father, if this cup may not pass away from me, except I drink it, thy will be done. And he came and found them asleep again: for their eyes were heavy. And he left them, and went away again, and prayed the third time, saying the same words. Then cometh he to his disciples, and saith unto them, `Sleep on now, and take your rest: behold, the hour is at hand, and the Son of man is betrayed into the hands of sinners. Rise, let us be going: behold, he is at hand that doth betray me'" (vv. 42-46).

There are spirits that we call a hereditary condition. A hereditary condition is different from a genetic condition. Genetic is chemical. A hereditary condition is something that is passed on from your parents and family members or associates. (See Proverbs 13:20.) A genetic trait is passed on at birth. If the father is blond, the son or daughter may be blond. You cannot change genetics. Hereditary traits are acquired. They manifest themselves later on in life. Read Genesis 20:1-2 and 26:7. Abraham lied about his wife and said she was his sister; so did his son Isaac and his grandson Jacob. Abraham was a believer; so were his sons, yet a lying spirit was transferred from the father to the son and to the grandson. The Bible tells us there are many voices in the world. But God has only one voice. God is the truth. Because He is truth, He speaks only the truth. The voice of the world comes in many shades and colors. It can be a deceiving voice, a lying voice, a hypocritical voice or a condemning voice. Then there is the human voice. The human voice can be used by demonic spirits or by God's Spirit. God can use man's voice to bring a message to the body. You and I can use our voices to communicate with others.

I may attempt to communicate with you, but you can choose to receive or not to receive. Many voices will try to speak to you concerning your relationship with other Christians or with God. You must learn the differences between them.

You can either accept failure, defeat and destruction or you can reject them. You do not have to receive the words they bring.

In order for spirits to be transferred, you have to be receptive, either willingly or ignorantly. The devil does not care which way he comes in. He just wants to come in.

Habakkuk 3:3-4 (NIV) says, "God came from Teman...rays flashed from his hand." Bright beams came out of Him. They showed where His power was—in His hands.

The devil was with God for many years prior to his fall. He knows that God has hands.

In Matthew 21 sinners tried to put their hands on Jesus, but because His time had not yet come, they were unable to. Even though people lay hands on you, their power (good or evil) will not enter you unless you allow it. What you do with that power depends on you. Many people are healed in a service, but before they walk out their symptoms return. This occurs because they are not able to retain the power that was transferred to them. Why? Because the devil knows if you keep the power, you are going to be healed. He does not like that. That is why the Bible says the devil comes immediately and steals the seed (the Word), lest you believe and be saved, delivered or healed.

When His time had come, Jesus knew He would be betrayed by one of His own people. Isn't it amazing how the devil still uses people within our own circles to betray us?

Money has power. Next to God, money is the most powerful thing. If you have money you can buy the world. He who has money pretty well controls the natural world. Money will find a way to cause problems. It causes problems in families, in business and in the church.

Jesus already said who the betrayer was. Why did Judas do it? We are not any different today from Judas. We like to sit in the background and criticize those who have gone before us. Judas loved Jesus, but Judas had a weakness: money. He did not put his security in the Lord. Judas knew that money was important. He was already weak.

Judas asked Jesus a question but he already knew the answer. He had already allowed that spirit to come in. The prince of the world was at work in him.

After Mary anointed Jesus' feet with ointment and wiped them with her hair, the aroma lingered in her hair. The same ointment that was on Jesus was on her. Do you see the importance of associating with Jesus? If you, then, being in the house of the Lord, have His anointing, joy and peace, will they remain with you when you leave? Will the aroma of Jesus and the glory of God follow you?

Mary could have used a towel. She could have used many things other than her hair, but she used her hair. By that anointing she was able to tell others that the aroma that was on Jesus was on her as well.

It appears that Judas was very concerned about the poor. Every time this type of person appears in the church and talks about the poor, I know exactly what spirit is in them and what they are like. It sounds very religious and noble that we should take care of the poor.

If people start criticizing you, accusing you of not taking care of the poor, you can see what kind of spirit they are motivated by. It is a selfish spirit. This is not to say we should not care for the poor. We should care for the poor, the widows and orphans.

There is a right way and a wrong way to minister to the poor. The poor will always be here. Some will never want to be anything but poor. They will express their gratitude at your generosity, but a month or a year later they will be in the same position they were before you gave to them. If you sell everything and give it to the poor, they will still be poor, and so will you.

The welfare program is not of God. I believe a church should minister to those who are needy, not those who are lazy. A spirit of poverty is real. When you understand the difference between the poor and the needy, you will be able to deal with them differently. A needy person may not be physically able to work, but he is willing to do whatever you ask of him. You help that person. A poor person wants everyone to feel sorry for him and give to him. The poor will not do anything for themselves or for anyone else. They will always give you a guilt trip.

Judas Iscariot was a thief. A thief always comes with a wrong spirit. He wants to transfer that spirit to you. I encourage you to be very sensitive to the Lord so that you will immediately be able to discern what kind of spirit is in a person. If what they say is not motivated by love, it is a wrong spirit. Anything Christians do must be motivated by love or it is not of God. I don't care how well-versed you are in the Scriptures. God is love, and everything He does is love.

The Bible is very clear about those who speak negatively. They want to transfer their misery to you. You do not need their misery. Any Christian who loves God will not allow himself to be used by the wrong spirit. You can find out immediately who they are by testing their spirit. Their gospel always comes with an attitude not in line with God's Word. If you talk to them long enough, you will detect their wrong spirit because it will manifest itself. God says that everything that is in secret will be brought to light.

CHAPTER EIGHTEEN

Standing Firm with God

Proverbs 26:22-28 says that when one's hatred is covered by deceit, his wickedness will be shown before the whole congregation. Those who have dislike for other people cover up through deceit, smooth talk, kind words and by winning confidence. They want you to be part of their conspiracy. David spoke about this. He said, "These people who are close to me have conspired against me." Because of the deceit in them, they thought they were smarter than anyone else. They rebelled against authority. They began to find fault in other people.

Those who are immature and weak, even if they love God, are attracted to smooth talkers. Smooth talkers flatter you with their lips. They use you as a tool that they can manipulate. You become a puppet to them. When you accomplish their purpose, they throw you away.

A person who lies does not really like you. It gives him pleasure to see you suffer. It gives him pleasure to see your business decline. It gives him pleasure to see your marriage break up. We must learn to discern such spirits. They are out to destroy.

Proverbs 28:25 says, "He that is of a proud heart stirreth up strife: but he that putteth his trust in the Lord shall be made fat." The proud person brings a spirit in the midst of a congregation which causes problems.

We must stop the thief. We must not allow that spirit to be transferred to Christians who are not able to discern for themselves what is happening.

God Has Never Failed: He Will Not Fail You

The Bible teaches that we must always keep our shield of faith up and protect one another. I need to protect you, and you need to protect me. If you have a question concerning something, come and ask me. If anyone says something to you, say, "Let's go find out. Let's not talk about it. Let's find the truth." If I have sinned or gone astray, help me get back on track instead of pushing me away. If a Christian is derailed, he is no good to anyone.

How many times will people say, "Oh, have I got a juicy tidbit for you!" They tell you it is juicy, something that tastes good.

These people have allowed a destructive, negative spirit to enter in. What they need is deliverance, but they do not want it. They enjoy the position they are in. I know it does not sound logical, but there are people who are maneuvered by the devil. They enjoy gossiping. They like to have titles and positions in high places. They want people to say, "Look how good he is." They are always talking about others.

Matthew 26:38-39 says, "Then saith [Jesus] unto them, My soul is exceeding sorrowful, even unto death: tarry ye here, and watch with me. And he went a little farther, and fell on his face, and prayed, saying, O my Father, if it be possible, let this cup pass from me: nevertheless not as I will, but as thou wilt."

Jesus had His own will, but He understood authority. He submitted Himself to authority and did not rebel against it. He came to do the will of the One who sent Him, His Father. Yet in His flesh He was struggling.

We too have a choice to make. Each individual must choose whether or not he is willing to allow God's Word to be the final authority in his life. God will not take your will from you. You must give it to Him. If you do not, someone else will control your will.

"And he cometh unto the disciples, and findeth them asleep, and saith unto Peter, What, could ye not watch with me one hour?" (v. 40). I am sure He was disappointed. Jesus was about to be crucified, and He knew it. He asked his disciples to pray with Him, to intercede for Him for strength, and they were sleeping. Jesus did not like sleepers in church. Neither do I. He said, "What? You could not wait for one hour?" He only had one hour of prayer, and they fell asleep.

"Watch and pray, that ye enter not into temptation: the spirit indeed is willing, but the flesh is weak" (v. 41). How true that is. Many of us desire to serve God, know more about God and read the Word of God. We have every intention of studying the Word. We even make preparations to read the Word before we get in bed. Once in bed you open your Bible, but you cannot keep your eyes open. You fall asleep. The spirit was willing, but the flesh took over. The Bible drops on the floor someplace, and you wake up three hours later and say, "What happened?"

It's just as true today as it was then. I am sure that the disciples were willing. They were with Him. They wanted to pray. I think we can all relate to that situation.

"He went away again the second time, and prayed, saying, O my Father, if this cup may not pass away from me, except I drink it, thy will be done. And he came and found them asleep again: for their eyes were heavy. And he left them, and went away again, and prayed the third time, saying the same words" (vv. 42-44).

You can see that Jesus was as persistent in praying as the disciples were persistent in sleeping. In His Spirit and in His soul He knew, so He kept on praying and asking the Father. His flesh was crying out.

"Then cometh he to his disciples, and saith unto them, Sleep on now, and take your rest: behold, the hour is at hand, and the Son of man is betrayed into the hands of sinners" (v. 45). We taught about God's having power in His hands. The devil also knows the power that is in his hands. Jesus said He was going to be betrayed into the hands of sinners.

"Rise, let us be going: behold, he is at hand that doth betray me. And while he yet spake, lo, Judas, one of the twelve, came, and with him a great multitude with swords and staves, from the chief priests and elders of the people. Now he that betrayed him gave them a sign, saying, Whomsoever I shall kiss, that same is he: hold him fast. And forthwith he came to Jesus, and said, Hail, master; and kissed him. And Jesus said unto him, Friend, wherefore art thou come? Then came they, and laid hands on Jesus, and took him" (vv. 46-50).

They put their physical hands on Him and took Him. "And, behold, one of them which were with Jesus stretched out his hand, and drew his sword, and struck a servant of the high priest's, and smote off his ear. Then said Jesus unto him, Put up again thy sword into his place: for all they that take the sword shall perish with the sword. Thinkest thou that I cannot now pray to my Father, and he shall presently give me more than twelve legions of angels? But how then shall the scriptures be fulfilled, that thus it must be?" (vv. 52-54).

The Bible says a legion is about six thousand. Twelve legions would be over seventy-two thousand angels. If one angel sets a thousand demons to flight and two set ten thousand to flight, there were not enough demons in the earth to set against Him. God would have sent the whole host of heaven to deliver Jesus if that was what He wanted. But Jesus came to fulfill the Scriptures. He was filled with the Spirit of God. No matter what the devil was doing, He knew God would not leave His soul in hell. It is good to know the promises of God. If you know the promises of God, you do not have to be afraid of what the devil throws your way. You cannot lose with God. If you know the end result, you can be bold in the presence of the devil.

"In that same hour said Jesus to the multitudes, Are ye come out as against a thief with swords and staves for to take me? I sat daily with you teaching in the temple, and ye laid no hold on me. But all this was done, that the scriptures of the prophets might be fulfilled. Then all the disciples forsook him, and fled" (vv. 55-56).

All Things Are Subject to Change Except God

David also said in the Psalms that everyone forsook Him and fled. He was by Himself. David knew and Jesus knew that all men forsook Him, even His disciples, but God the Father was with Him. He had confidence that God would never leave Him or forsake Him. Your confidence and mine should be as strong in God as His was. Stand fast in the Word of God, and God's promises will prevail. In the storms of life, problems and situations are temporary. They are subject to change, and they will change. You may have to endure for a while, but they will change. God's Word never changes.

The Bible says they all fled. My friend, let me ask you a question. Suppose the whole nation is against you. Suppose your whole family turns against you. Are you willing to stand on the Word and believe that God is with you? Suppose all your friends criticize you. Suppose all of society is against you. Are you willing to say as Jesus said, "Thou wilt not leave my soul in hell. I am going to trust You"? That is what God is looking for. God is looking for people who will trust in His ability to deliver them more than in the circumstances that seek to destroy their lives.

"And they that had laid hold on Jesus led him away to Caiaphas the high priest, where the scribes and the elders were assembled. But Peter followed him afar off unto the high priest's palace, and went in, and sat with the servants, to see the end" (vv. 57-58).

"Then did they spit in his face, and buffeted him; and others smote him with the palms of their hands, Saying, Prophesy unto us, thou Christ, Who is he that smote thee?" (vv. 67-68). They were mocking Him and beating Him. Peter was watching.

"And after a while came unto him they that stood by, and said to Peter, Surely thou also art one of them; for thy speech bewrayeth thee. Then began he to curse and to swear, saying, I know not the man. And immediately the cock crew. And Peter remembered the word of Jesus, which said unto him, Before the cock crow, thou shalt deny me thrice. And he went out, and wept bitterly" (vv. 73-75).

When people persecute you for Jesus' sake, it should be an honor. It should not be a shame. Because of the flesh, Peter denied Jesus. The Bible says Peter began to curse and swear saying, "I know not the man."

Christ wants us to be filled with His Spirit so that we can do a greater work for Him on this earth and be a blessing to the body of Christ.

CHAPTER NINETEEN

His Name Is Jesus

All through the Bible God tells His people not to fellowship with those who have wrong spirits. Since God has said this, it would be to our advantage to heed what He says. If we do not, we open ourselves to wrong spirits that will make our lives miserable. I am convinced that people who purpose to serve God, who are open to the Holy Spirit and seek after the truth, can eliminate many problems and much spiritual turmoil in their lives.

Even though there are problems all around us, we can get beyond those problems. Psalm 23 says that God will prepare for us a banquet table in the presence of our enemies. He is not afraid of the devil. That banquet table will provide whatever you need. God is not limited to french fries and greasy hamburgers. When God prepares a banquet table, rest assured it will be more than enough.

This banquet is not only for our spiritual being but also for our physical being. God wants our physical bodies to be strong, healthy and prosperous. The physical, outward appearance is what man looks on. God looks into the heart. When your heart is clean and pure, your physical body will also be clean and pure. That is what the world sees. Humanity is searching for answers. We have the answer. His name is Jesus.

When we walk in His Spirit we are not to be selfish and keep what we have for ourselves. Whatever wisdom we learn of the Holy Spirit we must be ready to share with those who are hungry. Sometimes people are not ready to receive what you have. You have to be wise, discerning when to share and when not to share. Sometimes people are ready for you to lay hands on them and transfer the healing power of God into their bodies. Sometimes they are not. Some people have allowed themselves to be sick so they can get the attention they have been craving. They need deliverance, but they do not know it.

There have been people in the prayer line who were brought by their relatives to be prayed for, and they said, "Don't pray for me. Don't touch me." They did not want to be healed.

To a person who loves God and enjoys health, it is difficult to grasp why anyone would want to be that way. You have to understand that they are prisoners. The only satisfaction they get is when people pay attention to them, feel sorry for them and pamper them as children. They do not want to receive healing; therefore, they do not want you to lay hands on them because power is transmitted through hands.

"And he entered into a ship, and passed over, and came into his own city. And, behold, they brought to him a man sick of the palsy, lying on a bed: and Jesus seeing their faith said unto the sick of the palsy; Son, be of good cheer; thy sins be forgiven thee" (Matt. 9:1-2).

Jesus did not lay hands on him. He spoke the Word, and healing power was transmitted to him.

Mark 2:2: "And straightway many were gathered together,

insomuch that there was no room to receive them, no, not so much as about the door: and he preached the word unto them."

Preaching the Word is what causes the power to be present. It is like an engine. If the engine is not running it does not produce power. The Word of God generates power, but you must put it into gear and act on that power so it can flow into you. If you are not willing to receive the power, you will not have the benefit of the power.

Luke 5:17-21 says, "And it came to pass on a certain day, as he was teaching, that there were Pharisees and doctors of the law sitting by, which were come out of every town of Galilee, and Judea, and Jerusalem: and the power of the Lord was present to heal them. And, behold, men brought in a bed a man which was taken with a palsy: and they sought means to bring him in, and to lay him before him. And when they could not find by what way they might bring him in because of the multitude, they went upon the house top, and let him down through the tiling with his couch into the midst before Jesus. And when he saw their faith, he said unto him, Man, thy sins are forgiven thee. And the scribes and the Pharisees began to reason, saying, Who is this which speaketh blasphemies? Who can forgive sins, but God alone?"

These men had simple faith that Jesus had power to heal them. The man who came was not a believer. He was a sinner who was full of palsy. Jesus said, "Because of your faith, thy sins be forgiven thee." We see then that sin and sickness have something in common. When Jesus forgave him his sins, and the man was set free, he got up, picked up his bed and walked. Jesus transmitted the power, but the man was willing to receive. When He taught the Word, there was power present to heal, but no one received it except one man who was sick of palsy, who was not even well-versed in the law. In preaching the Word, people receive deliverance, joy and peace.

Power by itself doesn't do much good unless authority goes with it. Authority doesn't do you any good unless you have the power to enforce it. For example, when a police officer wears his uniform and his badge, they represent his authority. Once he goes on duty he has the power to enforce that authority. The entire city, the mayor and the city council have given him the power and the authority to enforce the law. When that police officer stops a person who does something wrong, not only does he have the authority to stop him but he also has the power to take him to jail if need be. What good would it be if you had the authority of a police officer but you were not allowed to stop crime? As you can see, both authority and power are important.

The religious leaders recognized that when Jesus taught the Word, He had power and authority, but not as the scribes. The scribes had power, but they had no authority. These men recognized that Jesus was different. They had religion and authority, but they had no power over the devil, sickness or disease. Jesus had power and authority.

Everywhere He went, the first thing Jesus did was teach the Word. When I go into a dark room, the first thing I want to do is turn on the lights so I can see. Jesus, before He taught anything, turned the lights on. When He turned the lights on, He could see where the demons were, what to do with those demons and how to heal the sick. Before we can have the power of God working in and through our lives, before we can transfer any of the healing power, we have to turn our lights on. We have to have the Word in us. Teach the Word, even to those who are sick. You have to prepare them, and they have to be willing to hear.

Mark 1:22-24 says, "And they were astonished at his doctrine: for he taught them as one that had authority, and not as the scribes. And there was in their synagogue a man with an unclean spirit; and he cried out, Saying, Let us alone; what have we to do with thee, thou Jesus of Nazareth? art thou come to destroy us? I know thee who thou art, the Holy One of God."

When Jesus taught the Word, an unclean spirit cried out. When we teach the Word, it puts a pinch on demons. It also puts a pinch on the people who have the demons in them. It makes them so uncomfortable they leave the church. The demons will drive them out of the church. Those people cannot take the Word. Rather than turning the demons loose and asking for help, they run from the church. Demons hate the Word, which is Jesus of Nazareth.

Those demons in the synagogue recognized the power and authority of Jesus, and they acknowledged Him as being the Holy One of God.

If more Christians were half as smart as demons, they would realize where sickness, disease and torment come from. Jesus spoke to demons. That means demons are intelligent beings that understand language. You must speak with authority. You cannot say, "Maybe you better come out." That's not the way to drive demons out. They will jump on you and tear you apart as they did the sons of Sceva. But when you approach them full of God's Word and full of light, the demons come out. When your light shines, it causes demons to back away from you. The amount of illumination in your life depends on the Word present in you. That is why we must fill our minds with the Word.

By the same token, if you leave the lights on in a car without the engine running, the battery will run down. You will not have enough power to start the engine. If the Word is not charged up in you, your battery will go dead and you will not have enough power. That is when the devil comes. He looks for "weak batteries." A car that cannot run is abandoned. Thieves will steal the wheels, the engine and tear up the car. That is what happens in the natural: thieves come. The devil comes and strips God's temple when the people of God are not full of the power of God.

Jesus spoke to the demons and told them to be quiet. He had power to keep them quiet. "And when the unclean spirit had torn him [tormented him], and cried with a loud voice, he came out of him" (v. 26). Even though that demon did not want to go, he had no choice. When God said "Go!" he had to leave.

"And they were all amazed, insomuch that they questioned among themselves, saying, What thing is this? what new doctrine is this? for with authority commandeth he even the unclean spirits, and they do obey him" (v. 27).

Jesus did not lay His hands on them. He spoke the Word. The power Jesus had was stronger than the demonic power. When the power entered into the man who was tormented by a demon, the spirit went out, and the man was set free.

The devil is not impressed with your doctorate degree. He is not impressed by how many businesses you own. What he is impressed by is the Word in you. When you and I spend time with Jesus in His Word, the world will recognize there is something different about us, and we will do signs and wonders. There is power in the Word.

Demons have knowledge, and because they have knowledge, there is demonic activity. The Bible says Jesus would not allow them to speak because they knew Him. If they knew Him, they knew about Him. He would not allow these familiar spirits to talk.

Today there are people (and I know some who claim to be Christians) into supernatural things who use familiar spirits to get people to follow them. They have tremendous followings because people are attracted to the supernatural. Because they do not have knowledge of the Word, they are unable to discern between God's Spirit and demonic spirits. Fortunetelling is the domain of demonic spirits.

Occult activity is so real that people just fall into it. It is difficult for them to believe it is not of God. They have been deceived. They claim to be Christians. They speak in tongues. Just because a person speaks in tongues does not mean he is your brother or sister. I have seen a lot of tongue-talking liars, cheaters, backbiters and deceivers.

Demonic spirits are real. Be wise and do not allow the supernatural to influence you until you have discerned the source of the power. If it is demonic power, do not get involved or even fellowship with it. When you make yourself available, those spirits will hover over you until they get inside you.

After Jesus had done His great works, He had to build Himself up again. He had to refresh Himself. He took time away from the people. He went away to be with His Father and to pray. You cannot be with people all the time. Jesus loved people. If anybody loved people, Jesus did. But Jesus walked away from everybody to be alone with His Father. After He was refreshed spiritually, He could be used again by God to minister to the people.

"And in the morning, rising up a great while before day, he went out, and departed into a solitary place..." (v. 35). No phone numbers were given out. No one knew where He was going. Why would Jesus want to do that? Why would He want to get away from everybody? He needed to recharge His spirit.

"And when they had found him, they said unto him, All men seek for thee. And he said unto them, Let us go into the next towns, that I may preach there also: for therefore came I forth" (vv. 37-38).

"And he preached in their synagogues throughout all Galilee and cast out devils. And there came a leper to him, beseeching him, and kneeling down to him, and saying unto him, If thou wilt, thou canst make me clean. And Jesus, moved with compassion, put forth his hand, and touched him, and saith unto him, I will; be thou clean. And as soon as he had spoken, immediately the leprosy departed from him, and he was cleansed" (vv. 39-42).

Jesus saw the man's heart. He wanted to receive. Jesus did not go to him. He came to Jesus. On the other hand, Jesus went to Simon Peter's house where his mother-in-law was full of fever. She could not get up and go to Jesus, so He went to her and touched her. But this man could come, and he did. Jesus touched him. The power was transferred into him, and he was healed.

He Will Never Let You Down

Jesus taught His disciples not only by teaching the Word but also by demonstrating power. They were able to learn from this and have confidence and do as He did. The same power that was flowing through Him would flow through them.

When you know the Word and have confidence in it, demons and sickness have to obey. The problem is that our flesh hinders us from releasing that power because we think it might not work. How many of you have had that thought?

You may say, "But what if I lay my hands on them and they don't get any better?" If that is your problem, do not lay hands on anyone because nothing will happen. First get your mind stayed on Jesus; get your confidence built up. It is not your power anyway. It is from the Word. God said He has given us power, and His power always works.

Your mind needs to be renewed daily. Your spirit only needs to be saved, or born again, once, but your soul must be renewed daily by the Word of God. If you do not renew your mind, doubts will come in, saying, "What if it doesn't work?" We are still in the natural body, and the devil has access to the natural man.

Jesus said, "I will; be thou clean. And as soon as he had spoken, immediately the leprosy departed from him, and he was cleansed" (v. 42).

When you lay hands on a person, the power of God flows immediately into him. Before something manifests in the physical, it starts in the spirit. You may not feel tingling in your hands. Sometimes you do. Sometimes the feeling is so strong it is like putting your hand in boiling water. The power of God will flow into that person. As long as he is willing and open, healing will take place when you lay your hands on him because it is a spirit. The physical will catch up later on. Sometimes you can immediately see it in the physical as well. Sometimes a person who was deaf will be able to hear immediately. Sometimes you may see a lump disappear. You curse that thing, and it falls off immediately. Sometimes it doesn't. Does that mean God is not healing them? No!

This is where many people have difficulty. They look with their eyes and think nothing happened. Because they do not see any outward change, symptoms become more important to them than the Word. The Bible says out of the abundance of your heart your mouth will speak.

As people learn to trust the Word in spite of circumstances, in spite of what their eyes see, they realize the Word never fails. We constantly need to go back to the Word because that is where the power is. That is where the strength is. That is where the life is. If you keep speaking the Word, circumstances will change.

In Mark 2:2 Jesus preached the Word, which brought comfort, peace, joy, rejoicing, deliverance and healing to the spirit, soul and body. That is why we read in Isaiah 61:1-3 that Jesus came to heal the sick. Has He changed His mind today? Is He the same?

He Loves You Beyond Measure

Do you know it takes faith to get saved? Do you know it takes faith to get healed? Do you know it takes faith to be baptized in the Holy Spirit? If it takes faith to be healed, I would like to ask this question: Are there saved people today? Yes. So faith has not stopped working, has it? If people believe God's Word and have faith that God forgave their sins, how can we say that healing is not for today? How can we say that speaking in tongues is not for today when it takes faith? See how tricky the devil is? See how he has kept that power away from the believers who are not enjoying the fullness of God? God has not changed. We are all seeds of Abraham. What He gave to the first Christians, He gives to us today.

Luke 4:17-19 says, "And there was delivered him the book of the prophet Esaias. And when he had opened the book, he found

251

the place where it was written, The Spirit of the Lord is upon me, because he hath anointed me to preach the gospel to the poor; he hath sent me to heal the brokenhearted, to preach deliverance to the captive, and recovering of sight to the blind, to set at liberty them that are bruised, to preach the acceptable year of the Lord."

That is the ministry of Jesus. That is His whole ministry. That is why He came. How can we deprive Him of His ministry? Jesus is the same today! His power is still the same. His Word is still the same. Everything He had for them, He has for us. Why? Because He is not a respecter of persons.

When you go out in His name, it is the anointing of God on the Word that breaks the yoke of bondage. When you move in the Spirit, you will have Pharisees and Sadducees of today tell you, "It's not for everyone. It's not for today." Why? They are religious. They say they know God, but they deny the power thereof. The Bible says to turn away from them. That is our responsibility.

As long as your heart is right and you are seeking God, He will guide and direct you. You will get to a point where you stand up, take your first step and say, "I like this much better!" Then you will take another step. And another. Before long you will be running.

All of this starts as you grow. Patience and stability are important. Having the confidence that God is with you is important. Let us grow in spiritual stature that God may be glorified and build a strong foundation under our feet. If this happens, no matter what kind of storm comes, our house will not be blown away Mathew 7:24-25.